Steve Wohlberg

A Jewish believer exposes false prophecies about Israel, the temple, and Armageddon

Published by:
Amazing Discoveries
7051 McCart Avenue
Fort Worth, Texas 76133

Edited by Debra J. Hicks/Russ Holt
Proofread by Arlene Clark
Cover design by Allen Hrenyk/Craig Branham
Cover photo by Don Satterlee

ISBN 1-58019-139-8

FOREWORD
BY
DOUG BATCHELOR
DIRECTOR OF AMAZING FACTS
RADIO AND TELEVISION MINISTRIES

The Bible is a book for all people, but it revolves around a specific people, the Jews. It is impossible to have a clear picture of final events without first having a correct understanding of the true place of the Jewish nation in prophecy.

As a Jewish Christian, I am deeply concerned about the widely accepted distortions regarding modern Israel and prophecy. When Jesus came the first time, the Jewish people were not prepared to receive Him because they had misunderstood the prophecies regarding His kingdom. When He died on the cross, even His own disciples were bewildered. They were looking for a literal kingdom, in which the Messiah would overthrow their enemies so they could regain the earthly glory of Solomon's time. But when Jesus came the first time, He came to establish a spiritual kingdom (Luke 17:21).

Now, just before His second coming, the Christian world is repeating the Jewish nation's mistake. People are reversing the spiritual things to literal and then spiritualizing the plain letter! The tragedy is that in the process, they are setting themselves up for a devastating disappointment.

Steve Wohlberg courageously exposes these popular yet dangerous misconceptions in a clear and progressive style that is irrefutable for honest Bible students. Pray, read, and then hold onto your seat!

—DOUG BATCHELOR

TABLE OF CONTENTS

Chapter	Page

$\mathcal{A}$UTHOR'S $\mathcal{I}$NTRODUCTION

When January 1, 2000 finally arrived, it became obvious that doomsday prophecies about Y2K had failed. Earnest predictions about massive computer chaos, power disruptions, bank failures, stock markets crashing, nuclear missiles launching, and the resulting global terror, all proved to be false prophecies.

Is it possible that certain popular end-time prophecies about Israel will also fail?

On New Year's Eve, 1999, Israeli police assembled in record numbers inside Jerusalem. They were determined to keep the peace in the midst of growing concerns about terrorism and the possible explosive actions of religious fanatics. Hundreds of thousands of pilgrims and worshippers were crowding toward the Wailing Wall and the Temple Mount. News reporters from around the world swarmed throughout the City of David. With the approach of the long expected new millennium, apocalyptic interest was at its height. A lot of people were thinking, "If the arrival of the year 2000 has anything to do with the end of the world, then surely Jerusalem is the place to be!"

Yet nothing happened.

Why are the eyes of so many people fixed upon Jerusalem? There are many reasons, yet one big one is clear. The truth is that literally millions of Christians who are interested in Bible prophecy believe that earth's final events will one day center around the Middle East, Jerusalem, and the Jews. According to what is commonly understood, what happens to the nation of Israel is *very definitely* connected with the final battle of Armageddon, the return of Jesus Christ, and the end of the world.

The November 1, 1999 issue of *Newsweek*, in its comments about Y2K and Christian concerns, reported, "...the predominant issue in Christian prophecy is the return of the Jews to the Holy Land and the rebuilding of the Jerusalem temple..."[1]

Today, well-respected Christian scholars such as Hal Lindsey, Jack Van Impe, Dave Hunt, Peter Lalonde, Irvin Baxter Jr., and Tim LaHaye, all teach the significance of Israel in prophecy. The milestone Christian film, *Left Behind: The Movie*, which begins with a Russian surprise attack against Israel, continues this trend of associating the book of Revelation's end-time prophecies with a rebuilt Jewish Temple on the Temple Mount.

While there are differences of opinion among Christian scholars who teach about Bible prophecy, the majority firmly believe the following five events have been definitely predicted by God to occur before the second coming of Jesus Christ: (1) The rebirth of the state of Israel in 1948, (2) A soon coming "Seven Year Period of Great Tribulation," (3) The rebuilding of a third Jewish temple on the Temple Mount inside Jerusalem, (4) The rise of a mysterious man, the Antichrist, who will enter this rebuilt Jewish temple, proclaiming himself as God, (5) A final war against the nation of Israel, resulting in a Middle East battle of Armageddon.

It may sound like blasphemy to some, but the purpose of this book is to re-examine the accuracy of these popular teachings, in the light of Scripture.

Before we go any further, let me tell you a little about myself. I am Jewish, and I love Jewish people. I also believe Jesus Christ is my Messiah. Out of love for the human race, "Christ died for our sins." 1 Corinthians 15:3. He rose from the dead, and has ascended to heaven. He will one day return to this earth, as He promised, *and everything truly predicted in Bible prophecy will be fulfilled.* The battle of Armageddon will be fought. And yes, there will be an "end of the world." Matthew 24:14.

Yet I have come to a rather frightening conclusion. I am convinced that in the midst of today's popular prophetic teachings about the end-times, there are actually *gigantic errors* which are really not in harmony with the words of Jesus Christ or with the true meaning of the book of Revelation. The Master has warned us, "Take heed that no man deceive you." Matthew 24:4. I have taken this warning seriously.

Y2K prophecies have failed.

No terrorist explosions took place in Jerusalem on the eve of the new millennium.

You are about to discover solid New Testament proof that many Christian predictions about Israel will also fail.

The goal of this book is to *explode* these false prophecies, before it is too late.

Please read it prayerfully.

Its message could save your life.

¹Kenneth L. Woodward, "The Way the World Ends," *Newsweek*, Nov. 1, 1999, p. 73.

"AND HE GATHERED THEM TOGETHER
INTO A PLACE CALLED IN THE HEBREW TONGUE
ARMAGEDDON.

AND THE SEVENTH ANGEL
POURED OUT HIS VIAL INTO THE AIR;
AND THERE CAME A GREAT VOICE
OUT OF THE TEMPLE OF HEAVEN,
FROM THE THRONE, SAYING, IT IS DONE.

AND THERE WERE VOICES,
AND THUNDERS, AND LIGHTNINGS;
AND THERE WAS A GREAT EARTHQUAKE,
SUCH AS WAS NOT
SINCE MEN WERE UPON THE EARTH,
SO MIGHTY AN EARTHQUAKE, AND SO GREAT.

AND THE GREAT CITY WAS
DIVIDED INTO THREE PARTS,
AND THE CITIES OF THE NATIONS FELL:
AND GREAT BABYLON CAME
IN REMEMBRANCE BEFORE GOD,
TO GIVE UNTO HER THE CUP OF THE WINE
OF THE FIERCENESS OF HIS WRATH.

AND EVERY ISLAND FLED AWAY,
AND THE MOUNTAINS WERE NOT FOUND."

REVELATION 16:16-20

CHAPTER 1

WRESTLING WITH AN ANGEL

Have you ever heard of a wrestling match between a human being and an angel? As far as we know, it has happened only once in history. The details of this ancient story, which is recorded in Genesis chapter 32, will soon take on explosive significance in our study of Israel and Bible prophecy.

Abraham lived about 4,000 years ago. He eventually had a son named Isaac, then Isaac had a son named Jacob. It was Jacob who wrestled with the angel. As a result of that wrestling match, the angel changed Jacob's name to "Israel." In order to understand why this strange encounter took place and its deep meaning for us today, we must first study some history about Isaac, Rebekah, Esau, and Jacob as recorded in Genesis chapter 27.

"When Isaac was old, and his eyes were dim, so that he could not see," he decided to bless Esau, his firstborn son, before he died (Genesis 27:1-4). But first he sent Esau out to the field to hunt for a tasty meal. Isaac's wife, Rebekah, had other plans. Realizing the importance of her husband's "final blessing upon the firstborn," she coveted that blessing for her younger son, Jacob, who was more spiritual than Esau. While Esau was out hunting in the field, Rebekah quickly prepared a meal and convinced Jacob to take the food to Isaac while pretending to be Esau (Genesis 27:5-17).

When Jacob took the meal to his father, he lied, saying, "I am Esau thy firstborn; I have done according as thou badest me: arise, I pray thee, sit and eat of my venison, that thy soul may bless me." Verse 19. When Isaac inquired how it was that he had killed an animal so quickly, Jacob lied again, saying, "Because the Lord thy God brought it to me." Verse 20. Suspiciously, Isaac asked, "Art thou my very son Esau?" Jacob then lied a third time, saying, "I am." Verse 24. Isaac finally believed this deception and gave the firstborn's blessing to Jacob (verses 25-29).

Soon afterward Esau returned from his hunting trip, and then Isaac realized that he had been tricked. He said to Esau, "Thy brother came with subtilty, and hath taken away thy blessing." Verse 35. Then "Esau hated Jacob" and said in his heart, "I will slay my brother Jacob." Verse 41. However, Rebekah discovered Esau's plot and sent Jacob away to her relatives in a far country, where he remained for 20 years (Genesis 27:43; 31:41). Jacob never saw his mother again.

Genesis chapter 32 describes what happened to Jacob 20 years later on his journey back home. Surrounded by a large caravan of family and servants, Jacob sent messengers ahead of the group to tell Esau that he was coming. When these men returned with the news that Esau was on his way to meet them and that 400 soldiers were accompanying him, terror struck Jacob's heart. He felt a deep sense of guilt over his past sin of deception and was terrified for the safety of his family. So Jacob "rose up that night" and "was left alone" to plead with God for forgiveness and deliverance (Genesis 32:22, 24).

Then "there wrestled a man with him until the breaking of the day." Verse 24. Hosea 12:4 says this "man" was really an angel. Supposing that this might be his angry brother Esau, Jacob struggled for his life all night. Then, at the crack of dawn, this powerful stranger revealed himself, not as a foe, but as one sent from heaven. He touched Jacob's thigh, "and the hollow of Jacob's thigh was out of joint, as he wrestled with him." Verse 25.

Jacob suddenly realized that this powerful man was now possibly his only hope. Broken and helpless, he clung to him, saying, "I will not let thee go, except thou bless me."

"The angel then asked, "What is thy name?

"And he said, Jacob.

"And he said, Thy name shall be called no more Jacob, *but Israel*: for as a prince hast thou power with God and with men, and hast prevailed." Verses 26-28, emphasis added.

This is the first time the name "Israel" is used in the Bible. The context reveals its deep spiritual significance. In the beginning, "Israel" was a special name given to only one man, Jacob, by the angel of God. In the Bible, people's names mean more than they do today. Back then, names were often descriptions of people's characters. Jacob literally meant "Deceiver" or "Crook." When Esau discovered Jacob's sin of deception, he said to Isaac, "Is he not rightly named Jacob?" Genesis 27:36. Thus the name "Jacob" was a description of his character and of his sin. When the Angel said, "What is your name?" He already knew the answer. But He wanted Jacob to say his own name, which represented a humble confession and turning away from his sin. Jacob passed the test, repented, and placed his entire dependence upon God's mercy.

The response, "Thy name shall no more be called Jacob, but Israel," revealed that God had given him a new character! The word "Israel" literally means, "prince of God." Thus the name "Israel" was *a spiritual name*, symbolizing Jacob's spiritual victory over his past sin of deception. In other words, the man "Jacob" was now a spiritual "Israel." As we shall soon see, this truth about a spiritual Israel will take on explosive significance in our study of Israel and Bible prophecy.

Israel had 12 sons "which came into Egypt." Exodus 1:1-5. One son, named Joseph, had many dreams (Genesis chapter 37), and I will come back to this point later. The children of Israel multiplied in Egypt and were forced into slavery until the time of Moses. Then God told Moses, "Say unto Pharaoh, Thus saith the Lord, Israel is my son, even my firstborn. ... Let my son go." Exodus 4:22, 23. Here is an important development in biblical thought. The name "Israel" is now being expanded. It no longer refers only to Jacob, but also to his descendants. *The nation is now called "Israel."* Thus, the name "Israel" first applied to a victorious man, then to a people. It was God's desire that this new nation of Israel should also be victorious, as was Jacob, through faith in Him. God called this new nation of Israel, "my son ... my firstborn." Remember this. It will become significant later on in our study.

The next paragraph below contains little phrases about the nation of Israel which may seem dry to you at first. But amazing things can happen when you water a dry seed. Those little phrases will soon sprout and grow into trees of towering significance when we turn to the New Testament. Take special note of them.

Israel was called "a vine" that God brought "out of Egypt." Psalm 80:8. God said, "But thou, Israel, art my servant, ... the seed of Abraham." Isaiah 41:8. God also spoke of "Israel mine elect" in Isaiah 45:4. Again, God said through Isaiah, "Behold my servant, whom I uphold; mine elect, in whom my soul delighteth; I have put my spirit upon him: he shall bring forth judgment to the Gentiles. He shall not cry, nor lift up, nor cause his voice to be heard in the street. A bruised reed shall he not break, and the smoking flax shall he not quench: he shall bring forth judgment unto truth." Isaiah 42:1-3. All of these words originally applied to the nation of Israel. Don't forget that.

In about 800 B.C., the Lord said through the prophet Hosea, "When Israel was a child, then I loved him, and called my son out of Egypt." Hosea 11:1. Yet by this time the nation of Israel, which God loved, had failed to live up to the spiritual meaning of its own name. She had not lived victoriously, as a "prince of God." God sadly declared, "They sacrificed unto Baalim, and burned incense to graven images." Hosea 11:2. Yet God had a special plan. The sentence "When Israel was a child, then I loved him, and called my son out of Egypt" is actually like a time bomb. In Chapter 2 of this book, that verse will explode with tremendous importance as we turn to the New Testament.

CHAPTER 2

A NEW LOOK
AT JESUS CHRIST

In this chapter, we will begin to push the button that will explode the "Israel Deception."

Approximately 800 years had passed since the time of Hosea the prophet. Finally, heaven's prophetic clock struck twelve. Then "Jesus was born in Bethlehem of Judæa in the days of Herod the king." Matthew 2:1. Because King Herod felt threatened by this newly born potential rival to his throne, he sent soldiers who "slew all the children that were in Bethlehem." Matthew 2:16. Yet God warned Joseph in advance of the slaughter. "Behold, the angel of the Lord appeareth to Joseph in a dream, saying, Arise, and take the young child and his mother, and flee into Egypt, and be thou there until I bring thee word." Verse 13. So the family arose and "departed into Egypt." Verse 14.

The next sentence after Matthew 2:14 is like an atomic bomb in its prophetic implications. Under the inspiration of the Holy Spirit, Matthew wrote that

Joseph, Mary, and Jesus remained in Egypt "until the death of Herod: that it might be fulfilled which was spoken of the Lord by the prophet, saying, Out of Egypt have I called my son." Verse 15.

Do you realize what you just read? Matthew is quoting Hosea 11:1, which, in its historical context, referred to the nation of Israel being called out of Egypt in the time of Moses. Yet here the Gospel writer picks up this text and then declares it "fulfilled" in Jesus Christ! Here Matthew is beginning to reveal a principle that he develops throughout his book. The apostle Paul also taught the same principle, as we shall soon see.

Remember, the first time the name "Israel" is used in the Bible, it is a spiritual name given to one man, whose name was Jacob (Genesis 32:28). That name had to do with Jacob's spiritual victory. It means, "prince of God." Even so in the beginning of the New Testament that same name is beginning to be applied to one Man, to the Victorious One, to Jesus Christ, *the Prince of God*.

There are amazing parallels between the history of Israel and the history of Jesus Christ. In Hebrew history, a young man named Joseph, who had dreams, went to Egypt. In the New Testament we find another man named Joseph who had dreams and then went to Egypt. When God called Israel out of Egypt, He called that nation "my son." Exodus 4:22. When Jesus came out of Egypt, God said, "Out of Egypt I have called my son." When the nation of Israel left Egypt, the people went through the Red Sea. They were "baptized ... in the sea." 1 Corinthians 10:2. In the third chapter of Matthew, we read that Jesus was baptized in the Jordan river "to fulfill all righteousness." Verse 15. Then God called Jesus, "my beloved Son." Verse 17.

After the Israelites passed through the Red Sea, they spent 40 years in the wilderness. Immediately after Jesus was baptized in the Jordan river, He was "led up of the Spirit into the wilderness" for 40 days (Matthew 4:1, 2). At the end of the 40 days, Jesus resisted the devil's temptations by quoting three Scriptures. All were from Deuteronomy, the very book that God gave to Israel at the end of their 40 years in the wilderness! What does this mean? It means that in Matthew's book, Jesus is repeating the history of Israel, point by point, and is overcoming where they failed. He is becoming the new Israel, the Prince of God, the one victorious Man who overcomes all sin.

After healing a large number of people, Jesus "charged them that they should not make him known: That it might be fulfilled which was spoken by Esaias the prophet, saying, Behold my servant, whom I have chosen; my beloved, in whom my soul is well pleased: I will put my spirit upon him, and he shall shew judgment to the Gentiles. He shall not strive, nor cry;

neither shall any man hear his voice in the streets. A bruised reed shall he not break, and smoking flax shall he not quench, till he send forth judgment unto victory." Matthew 12:16-20.

Here Matthew is doing the same thing he did with Hosea 11:1. He is quoting Isaiah 42:1-3, which, in its original context, referred to God's "servant," which was "Israel ... my servant." Isaiah 41:8. Once again, under inspiration from the Holy Spirit, the writer of the first New Testament book declared that Isaiah 42:1-3 had been "fulfilled" by God's "servant," Jesus Christ!

What about those other seemingly dry little phrases about the nation of Israel? It is time to water them, too. They must now grow into trees that reach heaven. In Psalm 80:8, Israel was called a "vine." Yet Jesus Christ declared, "I am the true vine." John 15:1. God referred to the nation of Israel as "my son, even my firstborn." Exodus 4:22. Yet the apostle Paul later called Jesus Christ "the firstborn of every creature." Colossians 1:15. The prophet Isaiah called Israel "the seed of Abraham." Isaiah 41:8. Yet Paul wrote, "Now to Abraham and his seed were the promises made. He saith not, And to seeds, as of many; but as of one, And to thy seed, which is Christ." Galatians 3:16.

That last text is the clearest and most explosive of them all! In the Old Testament, God definitely called "Israel ... the seed of Abraham." Isaiah 41:8. Yet here Paul wrote that Abraham's seed does not refer to "many," but to "one, ... which is Christ." Thus we discover that, in the New Testament, what originally applied to the nation of Israel is now applied to Jesus Christ. The Messiah is now the "seed." Therefore, Jesus Christ is Israel!

Yet there is more. In Genesis and Exodus, the name "Israel" not only refers to one victorious man, to Jacob, but also to his descendants, who became Israel. The same principle is revealed in the New Testament. Right after the statement about Jesus being "the seed," Paul then told his Gentile converts, "And if ye be Christ's, then are ye Abraham's seed." Galatians 3:29. Thus in the New Testament, the name Israel not only applies to the one Victorious Man, the True Seed, Jesus Christ, but also to those who are in Christ. Believers in Jesus become part of "the seed." In other words, true Christians are now *God's spiritual Israel.*

God made a covenant with the twelve tribes of Israel at the foot of Mount Sinai. Animal sacrifices were offered. Then "Moses took the blood, and sprinkled it on the people, and said, Behold the blood of the covenant, which the Lord hath made with you." Exodus 24:8. At the end of His ministry, Jesus Christ made a new covenant with the twelve apostles in an upper room on Mount Zion. Before offering Himself as the great Sacrifice, our Lord declared, "This is my blood of the new testament [covenant], which is shed for many for the remission of sins." Matthew 26:28. What does this mean? It means that Jesus Christ, the True Seed, was there making a new covenant with a new Israel!

These fundamental New Testament facts will soon take on explosive significance when we examine what the book of Revelation *really teaches* about Israel, the temple, Babylon the Great, and Armageddon.

May I suggest you put your seatbelts on?

CHAPTER 3

*T*HE SHOCKING PRINCIPLE OF TWO ISRAELS!

Have you ever been hit so hard on the head that you started seeing double? Well, from what I have studied, the Christian world needs to get hit hard on the head with the truth of the New Testament! Then more Christians will start seeing double about the subject of Israel. According to the New Testament, there are now two Israels! The proof? Paul wrote, "They are not *all Israel,* which are *of Israel.*" Romans 9:6, emphasis added. In this chapter, we will discover that there is an Israel "according to the flesh" (Romans 9:3) and an "Israel of God" (Galatians 6:16) composed of both Jews and Gentiles who have personal faith in Jesus Christ.

Paul wrote, "Even as Abraham believed God, and it was accounted to him for righteousness. Know ye therefore that they which are of faith, the same are the children of Abraham." Galatians 3:6, 7. Paul's argument is that Abraham had faith, therefore those who have faith are his children. We might call this the concept of "faith lineage." This truth is like a key that can open a lock in our heads. Once the lock is open, then we can understand the shocking principle of two Israels.

John the Baptist understood and boldly preached the truth of "faith lineage." "In those days came John the Baptist, preaching in the wilderness." "But when he saw many of the Pharisees and Sadducees come to his baptism, he said unto them ..." "Think not to say within yourselves, We have Abraham to our father: for I say unto you, that God is able of these stones to raise up children unto Abraham. And now also the axe is laid unto the root of the trees: therefore every tree which bringeth not forth good fruit is hewn down, and cast into the fire." Matthew 3:1, 7, 9, 10.

Those Pharisees and Sadducees were part of Israel according to the flesh. They did not have faith like Abraham did, yet they thought they were his children. John the Baptist exposed this delusion. He thundered, "Don't think that!" John then laid the "axe" to the root of the trees by saying that if those men did not bear "good fruit" through faith like Abraham did, then they would be "hewn down, and cast into the fire." Verse 10. Thus natural lineage by itself is not enough. Without faith and a spiritual connection with God, those men were doomed.

Jesus Christ taught the same truth. A certain group of Jews once said to Him, "Abraham is our father."

Jesus responded, "If ye were Abraham's children, ye would do the works of Abraham." John 8:39. They claimed to be Abraham's children, but they had no faith. By saying, "If ye were Abraham's children," Jesus denied their claim. Christ continued, "But now ye seek to kill me, a man that hath told you the truth. This did not Abraham. Ye do the deeds of your father." John 8:40, 41.

They responded, "We have one Father, even God." Then "Jesus said unto them, If God were your Father, ye would love me: for I proceeded forth and came from God." "Ye are of your father the devil, and the lusts of your father ye will do. He was a murderer from the beginning, and abode not in the truth, because there is no truth in him. When he speaketh a lie, he speaketh of his own: for he is a liar, and the father of it." "He that is of God heareth God's words: ye therefore hear them not, because ye are not of God." John 8:41, 42, 44, 47.

What an atomic text! Here Jesus Christ Himself spoke words that blast into shivers a large portion of the prophetic theories currently held in the evangelical world. Jesus was talking to people who claimed to be Israelites, the children of Abraham. Yet they were only the Israel of the flesh! Jesus said they were not really Abraham's children at all. Because they had no faith and were following lies, their lineage actually went back to Satan, the father of lies! Soon we will separate

God's truth from Satan's lies when we look at what Revelation really teaches about Israel, the 144,000, Babylon, and Armageddon.

Jesus Christ also taught this same concept of "faith lineage" in John chapter 1. A spiritually minded Jew named Nathanael was wondering whether Jesus of Nazareth was really the Messiah. Retiring to a favorite spot under a fig tree, he prayed about the matter. Soon a friend introduced him to the Saviour. When Jesus saw Nathanael coming to Him, He said, "Behold an Israelite indeed, in whom is no guile!" John 1:47.

Nathanael had a natural lineage that went back to Abraham. Yet he had more. In his spiritual life, he had gained victories over guile, which means deception. When Jesus discerned Nathanael's spiritual lineage to Abraham and Jacob, He called him "an Israelite indeed." Therefore, just as the man Jacob became a spiritual Israel, even so had this man Nathanael become an Israelite indeed. He was part of God's true spiritual Israel.

Just as there are now two Israels, even so are there now two kinds of Jews. There are Jews in the flesh and Jews in the Spirit. In words of warning to certain Jews who were breaking the Ten Commandments, Paul wrote, "Behold, thou art called a Jew, and restest in the law, and makest thy boast of God." "For circumcision verily profiteth, if thou keep the law: but if thou be a breaker of the law, thy circumcision is made uncircumcision. Therefore if the uncircumcision [Gentiles] keep the righteousness of the law, shall not his uncircumcision be counted for circumcision?" "For he is not a Jew, which is one outwardly; neither is that circumcision, which is outward in the flesh: But he is a Jew, which is one inwardly; and circumcision is that of the heart, in the spirit, and not in the letter; whose praise is not of men, but of God." Romans 2:17, 25, 26, 28, 29.

Did you catch that? Someone who is "called a Jew" because he is a physical descendant of Abraham, and yet who lives as a lawbreaker, "is not a Jew." His "circumcision is made uncircumcision." To God, he is a Gentile. And the believing Gentile, who through faith keeps "the righteousness of the law," his uncircumcision is "counted for circumcision." Thus to God, he is a Jew. The teachings of John the Baptist, Jesus Christ, and Paul all agree that natural lineage is not enough. Whether or not someone is "an Israelite indeed" depends upon that person's faith and spiritual character. Paul summarized, "For we are the circumcision, which worship God in the spirit, and rejoice in Christ Jesus, and have no confidence in the flesh." Philippians 3:3. Anyone today can become one of these "Jews," even if their father was Adolf Hitler!

These concepts of "faith lineage," Jews being counted as Gentiles and Gentiles being counted as Jews, lead us into one of the biggest issues now facing the evangelical world. This issue is at the core of prophetic interpretation. In it we are faced with two options. One is the truth, the other a lie. One leads to heaven, the other, possibly, to hell.

The big question is "What about the promises God made to Israel in the Old Testament?" If we conclude that those promises must be fulfilled to the Israel of the flesh, then we must conclude that Jerusalem and the modern Jewish nation will eventually become the center of the final battle of Armageddon. But if we conclude that those promises can legitimately be fulfilled to God's Israel in the Spirit, then we must restudy the book of Revelation to discover how its end-time prophecies apply to Christians.

Paul deals with this highly explosive issue in Romans 9:2-8. His words require careful thought. With "continual sorrow" in his heart, Paul wrote about his Jewish "kinsman according to the flesh: Who are Israelites; to whom pertaineth the adoption, and the glory, and the covenants, and the giving of the law, and the service of God, *and the promises*." Verses 2-4, emphasis added. God did make promises to Israel in the Old Testament. Yet, what if some Jews do not believe in Him? Can God fulfill His promises to an unbelieving Israel in the flesh? If not, has His Word failed?

Paul's answer to these important questions is clear. "Not as though the word of God hath taken none effect.

For they are not all Israel, which are of Israel."
Verse 6. Notice that the concept of "two Israels" is
Paul's assurance that God's Word will not fail! Look
carefully: "They are not all Israel [the Israel of God],
which are of Israel [the Jewish nation]." Thus a Jew can
be of the Jewish nation, and yet not be part of the Israel
of God. Now, here is the highly explosive question. To
which Israel will God fulfill His promises?

Paul continues, "Neither, because they are the seed
of Abraham, are they all children: but, In Isaac shall thy
seed be called." Verse 7. Since not all physical
descendants of Abraham are automatically God's
children, therefore His promises are for those "in Isaac."
Abraham had two sons. The first was Ishmael, who was
born after the flesh. The second was Isaac, who was
born when Abraham had faith in God's promise
(Genesis 16:1-3, 15; 21:1-3; Romans 4:18-21). In
Galatians 4:22-31, Paul reveals that Ishmael *represents*
unbelieving Jews, while Isaac *represents* both Jews and
Gentiles who have faith! "Now we, brethren, as Isaac
was, are the children of promise." Galatians 4:28. The
children of promise are those who "receive the promise
of the Spirit through faith." Galatians 3:14. Therefore,
the Israel that is "in Isaac" is the Israel of God in the
Spirit!

Paul concludes, "That is, They which are the
children of the flesh, these are not the children of God:
but the children of the promise are *counted* for the

seed." Romans 9:8, emphasis added. Here is a summary of Paul's reasoning: (1) In the Old Testament, God made promises to "the seed of Abraham," (2) This "seed" would continue "in Isaac," (3) Isaac was born through faith, (4) Isaac represents those who have faith, (5) All who have faith—Jews and Gentiles—"are counted for the seed," (6) This seed is the "Israel" of God, (7) God will fulfill His promises *to this Israel,* and (8) Therefore, "the word of God" to Israel has not been made of "none effect," even though some natural Jews do not believe!

Thus we have the answer to the issue that means so much in prophetic interpretation. The Bible is clear. God will fulfill His Old Testament promises to those "in Isaac," that is, to His Israel in the Spirit. Those who are only "the children of flesh, *these are not the children of God:* but the children of the promise are counted for the seed." Romans 9:8, emphasis added. We should not expect God to fulfill His promises to an unbelieving Israel in the flesh, unless, of course, those natural Israelites choose to believe in Jesus Christ.

We will examine one more atomic section before we close this chapter. What about Paul's question, "Hath God cast away his people?" Romans 11:1. This verse is being quoted around the world to prove that God has not cast away the Israel of the flesh. Yet notice Paul's answer: "God forbid. For I also am an Israelite, of the seed of Abraham." Notice that Paul uses himself as an example to prove that God has not "cast away his people." Who are "his people"?

In the next three verses, Paul refers to ancient Israel's apostasy in the days of Elijah. God said to Elijah, "I have reserved to myself seven thousand men, who have not bowed the knee to the image of Baal." Verse 4. In Elijah's time there were also two Israels. One followed Baal, while the other followed God. Then Paul made this application. "Even so then at this present time also there is a remnant according to the election of grace." Verse 5. Just as in Elijah's time there was a faithful remnant of Israel, even so in Paul's time there was also a faithful remnant of believing Jews, who, like himself, had been saved by grace. These are God's people. It is *this faithful remnant of spiritual Israel* whom God has certainly not "cast away."

Soon we will see this exact issue addressed in the book of Revelation. As in the days of Elijah, we are now in the midst of a terrible apostasy. Yet today God has His "seven thousand" who have not "bowed the knee to Baal." They are His faithful remnant, *His Israel in the Spirit.* Like Elijah, they will be on the side of Jesus Christ and the truth at Armageddon!

CHAPTER 4

"CHOICE" AND THE CHOSEN NATION

From the top of Mount Sinai, the Almighty said to Moses: "Thus shalt thou say to the house of Jacob, and tell the children of Israel; Ye have seen what I did unto the Egyptians, and how I bare you on eagles' wings, and brought you unto myself. Now therefore, if ye will obey my voice indeed, and keep my covenant, then ye shall be a peculiar treasure unto me above all people: for all the earth is mine: And ye shall be unto me a kingdom of priests, and an holy nation." Exodus 19:3-6.

Notice the words "if" and "then." God said that "if" Israel obeyed, "then" they would be His peculiar treasure. That tiny word "if" involves a big issue. That word has to do with *conditions*. God loved Israel. He chose them apart from any obedience on their part. He brought them out of Egypt, bore them on eagles' wings, and brought them to Himself. Yet, contrary to popular opinion, God's use of the word "if" made it clear that the continuation of His favor to the Israelites was conditional upon their response to His goodness, upon their choices to obey. In other words, the members of the chosen nation must themselves choose correctly, or the consequences would be disastrous!

Forty years later, Israel entered the Promised Land and remained there for about 800 years. During this period, many responded to God's love by obeying His voice. But the majority strayed from the path of righteousness. Again and again, God manifested His mercy by raising up prophets and pleading with Israel to return to the covenant. Yet apostasy continued and deepened. Finally, after hundreds of years of warning, disaster struck. In 722 B.C., the northern tribes were carried away by the cruel Assyrians. In 586 B.C., Judah was taken to Babylon. Such was the result of wrong choices.

In 586 B.C., the armies of Babylon demolished Jerusalem and burned the temple with fire. The Jews were removed from their land and carried into captivity. Yet, in the mercy of God, this exile was not to be permanent. The prophet Jeremiah predicted that God "would accomplish seventy years in the desolations of Jerusalem." Daniel 9:2. After 70 years the Jews would leave Babylon, return to their land, and rebuild their temple and their city. God had decided to give His chosen nation another chance to respond to His love.

In simple terms, the Lord was saying: "You blew it. Let's try again!"

This "second chance" granted to the nation of Israel is revealed in the prophecy of the "seventy weeks." Near the end of the Babylonian captivity, the angel Gabriel told Daniel, "Seventy weeks are determined upon thy people and upon thy holy city, to finish the transgression, to make an end of sins, and to make reconciliation for iniquity, and to bring in everlasting righteousness, and to seal up the vision and the prophecy, and to anoint the most Holy." Daniel 9:24. This 70-week period was "determined" for Daniel's people, the nation of Israel. During that period, the chosen nation would have another opportunity to come into harmony with God. Near the end of this period, something big would happen. The Messiah would come "to bring in everlasting righteousness." As we shall see in Chapter 6, Israel's destiny as a nation would at that time be determined by her choice to receive or reject that Messiah!

Math was never my favorite subject in school. Yet we must apply ourselves to some mathematics in order to understand this particular prophecy.

70 weeks = 490 days

God said to Ezekiel, who was a contemporary of Daniel, "I have appointed thee each day for a year." Ezekiel 4:6. The 70-week prophecy must be "a day for a year" because it would reach down hundreds of years to the coming of the Messiah. Thus 490 days equals 490 years. When did it start? Gabriel tells us in the next verse, "Know therefore and understand, that from the going forth of the commandment to restore and to build Jerusalem unto the Messiah the Prince shall be seven weeks, and threescore and two weeks." Daniel 9:25.

Persia conquered Babylon in 538 B.C. Then King Cyrus issued a decree for the Jews to return to their land and to rebuild their temple (Ezra 1:1-3). Later, King Darius issued another decree that led to the completion of the temple (Ezra 6:1, 8). Still later, King Artaxerxes gave Nehemiah permission to rebuild the wall around the city (Nehemiah 1:3; 2:1-9). Yet the predicted "commandment to restore and to build Jerusalem" did not occur until Persian King Artaxerxes issued a lengthy decree giving Ezra official authority to "set magistrates and judges" over Jerusalem and to "execute judgment" upon all who refused to follow the laws of God and the king (Ezra 7:21, 25, 26). This was the only decree which fully restored civil authority to Jerusalem and to the Jewish state.

That commandment occurred "in the seventh year of Artaxerxes." Ezra 7:7. The date was 457 B.C., as many Bibles state in the margin of Ezra chapter 7. Gabriel said, "From the going forth of the commandment to restore and to build Jerusalem unto the Messiah the Prince shall be seven weeks [49 years], and threescore and two weeks [434 years]." Daniel 9:25.

49 years + 434 years = 483 years

Going forward 483 years from 457 B.C. comes to A.D. 27, the time of "the Messiah the Prince." The word "Messiah" means "Anointed One." In A.D. 27, which was the very year specified in prophecy, Jesus Christ was "anointed" by the Holy Spirit at His baptism (Matthew 3:16, 17; Acts 10:38)! Then Jesus said, *"The time is fulfilled,* ... repent ye, and believe the gospel." Mark 1:15, emphasis added. Jesus knew that He was fulfilling the prophecy of Daniel chapter 9!

The total period mentioned by Gabriel in Daniel 9:24 was "seventy weeks," or 490 years. Gabriel then subdivided this total period into three smaller periods— 7 weeks (verse 25), 62 weeks (verse 25), and 1 week (verse 27).

7 weeks + 62 weeks + 1 week = 70 weeks

We have seen that 7 weeks plus 62 weeks brings us down to A.D. 27, the time of Christ's anointing as the Messiah. That leaves one final week of the prophecy. Gabriel said, "He shall confirm the covenant with many for one week." Daniel 9:27. One week equals 7 days, which means 7 years. This famous 7-year period is often called "the 70th week of Daniel." In the next chapter, we will focus our attention on this controversial 70th week.

CHAPTER 5

THE "70TH WEEK OF DANIEL" DELUSION

In 1945, after months of agonizing deliberation, President Harry Truman finally decided to drop an atomic bomb upon Japan. Right or wrong, the ultimate goal of his decision was to end World War II and to prevent the death of millions. So, on August 6, a bomb called the "Little Boy" fell on Hiroshima. Three days later, another bomb called the "Fat Man" dropped on Nagasaki. Approximately 130,000 people were instantly vaporized. Many have argued whether or not it was the right thing to drop those bombs. But in the minds of those who made that decision, it was for the ultimate good of America.

Dear friend, it is for the ultimate good of the entire evangelical world for God's bomb of truth to now drop upon a gigantic prophetic delusion that is presently believed by millions. It is time to drop the "Little Boy." We will save the "Fat Man" for a later chapter.

The Bible says, "He shall confirm the covenant with many for one week: and in the midst of the week he shall cause the sacrifice and the oblation to cease." Daniel 9:27.

Have you ever heard of the "seven-year period of great tribulation"? The whole idea is rooted in two words of the above sentence! The two words are "one week." Supposedly, that period of "one week" applies to a final seven-year period of great tribulation at the end of time. Right now, all over planet Earth, in books, in magazines, in videos, on the radio, in seminaries, on the Internet, and at Bible prophecy conferences, Christians are talking about events they firmly believe will occur during that final seven years of tribulation.

According to the popular interpretation of Daniel 9:27, the "he" refers to a future Antichrist who will eventually make a covenant, or peace treaty, with the Jews during the final seven years of tribulation. In the "midst" of this tribulation, this Antichrist will cause "the sacrifice ... to cease." In order for the sacrifices to cease, they must have been restarted. Therefore, according to countless modern interpreters, there must be a rebuilt third Jewish temple on the Temple Mount in Jerusalem.

A popular Christian magazine called *Endtime* reflects this current view: "Three and one-half years after the confirming of the covenant [by the Antichrist] the Jews' Third Temple must be completed and sacrifice and oblation be in progress. We know this because Daniel 9:27 states that in the middle of the seven years the Antichrist will cause the sacrifice and the oblation to stop."[1]

Much of the Christian world is now locked in a fierce debate about whether Jesus will return for His church before the 7 years (the pre-tribulation view), in the midst of the 7 years (the mid-tribulation view), or at the end of the 7 years (the post-tribulation view). Yet by far the most explosive question, which few seem to be asking, should be "Is an end-time 'seven-year period of great tribulation' really the correct interpretation of Daniel 9:27 in the first place?"

Historically, Protestant scholars have not applied Daniel 9:27 to a future period of tribulation at all! Neither have they applied the "he" to the Antichrist. Rather, they applied it to Jesus Christ! Notice what the world-famous Bible commentary written by Matthew Henry says about Daniel 9:27: "By offering himself a sacrifice once and for all he [Jesus] shall put an end to all the Levitical sacrifices."[2] Another famous Bible commentary, written by Adam Clarke, says that during the "term of seven years," Jesus would "confirm or ratify the new covenant with mankind."[3] Finally, another well-respected old commentary declares: "He shall confirm the covenant—Christ. The confirmation of the covenant is assigned to Him."[4]

The following 10 points provide logical and convincing evidence that the "one week" spoken of in Daniel 9:27 does not apply to any future seven-year period of tribulation at all. Rather, this great prophetic period has already been definitely fulfilled in the past!

1. The entire prophecy of Daniel 9:24-27 covers a period of "seventy weeks." This period applies to one complete, sequential block of time. This prophecy would start during the Persian period and would end during the time of the Messiah.

2. Logic requires that the 70th week follow immediately after the 69th week. If it does not, then it cannot properly be called the 70th week!

3. It is illogical to insert a 2,000-year gap between the 69th and the 70th week. No hint of this gap is found in the prophecy itself. There is no gap between the first 7 weeks and the following 62 weeks. Why insert one between the 69th and the 70th week?

4. Daniel 9:27 says nothing about a seven-year period of tribulation, or about any Antichrist.

5. The focus of this prophecy is the Messiah, not the Antichrist. Modern interpreters have applied "the people of the prince" who would come to "destroy the city and the sanctuary" (verse 26) to the Antichrist. Yet the text does not say this. In the past, that sentence has

been applied to the Romans, who under Prince Titus did "destroy the city and the sanctuary" in A.D. 70.[5]

6. "He shall confirm the covenant." Jesus Christ came "to confirm the promises made unto the fathers." Romans 15:8. Nowhere in the Bible is Antichrist ever said to make or confirm a covenant with anyone! The word "covenant" *always applies* to the Messiah, never to the Antichrist!

7. "He shall confirm the covenant with many." Jesus said, "This is my blood of the new testament, which is shed for many." Matthew 26:28. Jesus used the same words, because He knew that He was fulfilling Daniel 9:27!

8. "In the midst of the week he shall cause the sacrifice and the oblation to cease." The 70th week was from A.D. 27 to 34. After three and a half years of ministry, Christ died in A.D. 31, "in the midst [middle] of the week." At the moment of His death, "the veil of the temple was rent [torn] in twain from the top to the bottom." Matthew 27:51. This act of God signified that all animal sacrifices had at that moment ceased to be of value. The Great Sacrifice had been offered!

9. "For the overspreading of abominations he shall make it desolate." Jesus plainly applied this "abomination of desolation, spoken of by Daniel the prophet" (Matthew 24:15) to the time when His followers were to flee from Jerusalem before the

destruction of the second temple in A.D. 70. Jesus told His 12 disciples, *"When ye shall see* Jerusalem compassed with armies [the Roman armies led by Prince Titus], then know that its *desolation* is near." Luke 21:20, emphasis added. Those disciples did "see" those very events. Christ's very last words to the Pharisees from inside the second temple were, "Behold, your house is left unto you desolate." Matthew 23:38. Thus Daniel's prophecy about Jerusalem becoming "desolate" was exactly fulfilled in A.D. 70! Jesus understood this perfectly.

10. Gabriel said that the 70-week prophecy specifically applied to the Jewish people (Daniel 9:24). From A.D. 27 to A.D. 34, the disciples went only "to the lost sheep of the house of Israel." Matthew 10:6. At the end of the 70 weeks, in the year A.D. 34, Stephen was stoned by the Jewish Sanhedrin (Acts chapter 7). Then the gospel began to go to the Gentiles. In Acts chapter 9, Saul became Paul, "the apostle of the Gentiles." Romans 11:13. Then in Acts chapter 10, God gave Peter a vision revealing that it was now time to preach the gospel to the Gentiles (Acts 10:1-28). Read also Acts 13:46.

The explosive evidence is overwhelming! Point by point, the events of the 70th week have *already been fulfilled in the past!* The following eight words found in Daniel 9:27: "confirm ... covenant ... many ... midst ... sacrifice ... cease ... abominations ... desolate" all find a perfect fulfillment in Jesus Christ and in early Christian history.

One reason why the Jewish nation as a whole failed to receive its Messiah was because its leaders and scholars failed to correctly interpret the 70-week prophecy. They failed to see Jesus Christ as the Messiah who *died* in the midst of the 70th week. The same thing is happening today! Amazingly, sincere Christian scholars are now misinterpreting the very same prophecy.

The entire "seven-year period of great tribulation" theory is a grand illusion. It may go down in history as the *biggest evangelical misinterpretation* of the 20th century! It can be compared to a big, fat hot air balloon. Inside, there is no substance, only air. As soon as Daniel 9:27 is understood correctly and the pin of truth is inserted, the balloon will pop. The fact is that no text in the Bible teaches any "seven-year period of great tribulation." If you look for it, you will end up like Ponce de Leon, who tirelessly searched for the famous fountain of youth but never found it.

The current debate and tremendous confusion over pre-tribulation, mid-tribulation, or post-tribulation is really a smoke screen of the enemy which is hiding the real issue. What is the real issue? We will find out when we study what the book of Revelation actually teaches about Israel, the temple, Babylon the Great, and Armageddon.

[1]Irvin Baxter, Jr., "Have the Final 7 Years Begun?" *Endtime* Magazine, May/June 1997, p. 17.

[2]*Matthew Henry's Commentary on the Whole Bible,* Vol. IV—Isaiah to Malachi, Complete Edition (New York: Fleming H. Revell Co.) 1712, notes on Daniel 9:27, p. 1095.

[3]*The Holy Bible* with a commentary and critical notes by Adam Clarke, Vol. IV—Isaiah to Malachi (New York: Abingdon-Cokesbury Press), notes on Daniel 9:27, p. 602.

[4]Rev. Robert Jamieson, Rev. A.R. Fausset, and Rev. David Brown, *A Commentary Critical and Explanatory on the Whole Bible,* Complete Edition (Hartford, Conn.: S.S. Scranton Co.), notes on Daniel 9:27, p. 641.

[5]See notes on Daniel 9:26 in commentaries by Matthew Henry (p. 1095), Adam Clarke (p. 603), and Jamieson, Fausset and Brown (p. 641).

CHAPTER 6

THE DIVINE DIVORCE

Then came Peter to him, and said, Lord, how oft shall my brother sin against me, and I forgive him? till seven times? Jesus saith unto him, I say not unto thee, Until seven times: but, Until seventy times seven." Matthew 18:21, 22. Jesus always chose His words carefully. His response to Peter contains an important lesson. "Seventy times seven" equals 490, which is a perfect reference to the 70-week prophecy of Daniel chapter 9!

The 70-week period in Daniel 9:24-27 represented a second opportunity for the chosen nation to demonstrate faithfulness to God. Israel's first temple had been destroyed and her children carried to Babylon because she had rejected the warnings God had given by His prophets. Yet through divine love and mercy, another opportunity would be granted to come into harmony with God. Israel returned to her land and built a second temple.

Though she had sinned at least "seven times," God's forgiveness toward the nation was extended to "seventy times seven." Near the close of this period, Someone greater than the prophets would come. Then Israel's destiny as a nation would be determined by her response to God's Son.

Near the end of Jesus Christ's earthly life, He beheld Jerusalem "and wept over it, Saying, If thou hadst known, even thou, at least in this thy day, the things which belong unto thy peace! but now they are hid from thine eyes. For the days shall come upon thee, that thine enemies shall cast a trench about thee, and compass thee round, and keep thee in on every side, And shall lay thee even with the ground, and thy children within thee; and they shall not leave in thee one stone upon another; because thou knewest not the time of thy visitation." Luke 19:41-44.

When Jesus spoke to Peter about forgiveness being extended "until seventy times seven," He knew that the 70-week prophecy was soon to end. He knew the significance of this prophecy to Israel as a nation, to Jerusalem, and to the second temple. Chapters 21-23 of Matthew reveal the sad, final, and explosive encounters between Jesus Christ and the leaders of His chosen people. It is now time to see the true meaning of those encounters.

During the week prior to His crucifixion, Jesus "went into the temple of God, and cast out all them that sold and bought in the temple, and overthrew the tables of the moneychangers, and the seats of them that sold doves, And said unto them, It is written, My house shall be called the house of prayer; but ye have made it a den of thieves." Matthew 21:12, 13. At this point, Jesus still called the second temple "My house." But a change would come.

"In the morning as he returned into the city, he was hungered. And when he saw a fig tree in the way, he came to it, and found nothing thereon, but leaves only, and said to it, Let no fruit grow on thee henceforward for ever. And presently the fig tree withered away." Verses 18, 19. Here the fig tree was a symbol of the Jewish nation. The "seventy times seven" countdown was nearing its close.

"When he was come into the temple, the chief priests and the elders of the people came unto him as he was teaching." Verse 23. Their plan was to expose Jesus as a false Messiah and then put Him to death. Jesus told those leaders a parable that outlined the entire history of Israel in one sweep. "There was a certain householder [God], which planted a vineyard [Israel], and hedged it round about [God's love], and digged a winepress in it, and built a tower [the temple], and let it out to husbandmen [the Jewish leaders], and went into a far country. And when the time of the fruit drew near, he sent his servants [the prophets] to the husbandmen, that they might receive the fruits of it. And the husbandmen took his servants, and beat one, and killed another, and stoned another. Again, he sent other servants more than the first [continued mercy]: and they did unto them likewise. But *last of all* he sent unto them his son [at the close of "seventy times seven"], saying, They will reverence my son. But when the husbandmen saw the son, they said among themselves, This is the heir; come, let us kill him, and let us seize on his inheritance. And they caught him, and cast him out of the vineyard, and slew him [their final sin]." Verses 33-39, emphasis added.

Then Jesus asked those leaders, "When the lord therefore of the vineyard cometh, what will he do unto those husbandmen? They said unto him, He will miserably destroy those wicked men, and will let out his vineyard unto other husbandmen, which shall render him the fruits in their seasons." Verses 40, 41. Did they realize what they were saying? Hardly! They had just pronounced their own doom!

Looking His murderers straight in the eye, Jesus sadly declared in words of burning truth, "Therefore I say unto you, The kingdom of God shall be taken from you, and given to a nation bringing forth the fruits thereof." Verse 43. The Master Himself said it. The kingdom of God would soon be "taken" away from an unbelieving Israel in the flesh and given to another "nation." Why? *Because of their final sin of crucifying "the Son"* (verses 38, 39).

In His next parable, Jesus outlined the same historical sequence but added details of the destruction of Jerusalem and the call of the Gentiles. "The kingdom of heaven is like unto a certain king, which made a marriage for his son, And sent forth his servants to call them that were bidden to the wedding: and they would not come. Again, he sent forth other servants, saying, Tell them which are bidden, Behold, I have prepared my dinner: my oxen and my fatlings are killed, and all things are ready: come unto the marriage. But they made light of it, and went their ways, one to his farm, another to his merchandise: And the remnant took his servants, and entreated them spitefully, and slew them. But when the king heard thereof, he was wroth: and he sent forth his armies, and destroyed those murderers, and burned up their city." Matthew 22:2-7. This literally took place when Jerusalem and the second temple were destroyed by the Romans in A.D. 70. Daniel's prophecy was fulfilled that said: "The people of the prince that shall come shall destroy the city and the sanctuary." Daniel 9:26. Continuing the parable, Jesus said, "Then saith he to his servants, The wedding is ready, but they which were bidden were not worthy. Go ye therefore into the highways, and as many as ye shall find, bid to the marriage." Matthew 22:8, 9. Thus Christ represented the call of the Gentiles at the end of the 70 weeks.

Matthew chapter 23 contains the Saviour's final words in tears and agony over His chosen people. Eight times during His last public exchange with Israel's leaders, Jesus cried out, "Woe to you, scribes and Pharisees, hypocrites!" Finally, with a broken heart, the Son of the Infinite God declared: "O Jerusalem,

Jerusalem, thou that killest the prophets, and stonest them which are sent to thee, how often would I have gathered thy children together, even as a hen gathereth her chickens under her wings, and ye would not! Behold, your house is left unto you desolate." Matthew 23:37, 38. This time God was not saying: "You blew it. Let's try again." Israel's decision to crucify Christ would have permanent consequences. The result was a searing separation—a painful, divine divorce.

Then "Jesus went out, and departed from the temple [He never returned]: and his disciples came to him for to show him the buildings of the temple. And Jesus said unto them, See ye not all these things? Verily I say unto you, There shall not be left here one stone upon another, that shall not be thrown down." Matthew 24:1, 2. In A.D. 70, the second temple was destroyed by the Romans, and more than one million Jews perished. Such was the terrible results of that divine divorce. Today, the Muslim Dome of the Rock stands on the Temple Mount. Will there be a third temple?

According to Daniel 9:24-27 and the teachings of Jesus Christ, the prophecy of "seventy times seven" represented the limits of national forgiveness for the Jewish nation—as a nation. What would happen next? A new day had come. It was time for the wall to come tumbling down.

CHAPTER 7

WHEN THE WALL CAME TUMBLING DOWN

In 1989, the Berlin Wall came down. Today there is nothing left of it. No longer is there a physical separation between East and West Germany. The two have become one. According to the Bible, this is exactly what Jesus Christ accomplished for Jews and Gentiles. As it is written, "For he is our peace, who has made both one, and has broken down the middle wall of partition between us." Ephesians 2:14.

The truth of the New Testament is often quite different from what is taught in seminaries and discussed in theological circles. One of the biggest areas of confusion concerns the issue of Jews and Gentiles. Many have been taught that God has two separate plans—one for the Jews, the other for the Gentiles. God's plan for the Gentiles is often seen as being fulfilled in "the church age." This idea of "two plans" is now being taught all over the world. Yet the big question is, "Does the New Testament really teach this popular two-plan theory?"

First, we must back up a little. The ending of the "seventy times seven," those woes on the Pharisees, the transfer of the kingdom, the divine divorce, and the destruction of the second temple did not mean that all Israel had rejected its Messiah! Nor is it fair to simply say, "The Jews killed Christ." No! This idea has terribly, unjustly, and cruelly fueled anti-Semitism for almost 2,000 years. It was not "the Jews" who killed Christ. It was human nature. It was your nature and mine. Jesus Christ died "for the sins of the whole world." 1 John 2:2.

Many Jews welcomed their Messiah. The 12 disciples were all Jewish. The Holy Spirit on the day of Pentecost fell only on Jews. It was 3,000 Jews who were then baptized (Acts 2:5, 22, 36, 41, 46). The early Church in Jerusalem was Jewish. Soon "a great company of the priests were obedient to the faith." Acts 6:7. With the exception of Luke, the entire New Testament was written by Jews. The question must be asked, "Should we call this group of early Jewish believers in Jerusalem 'Israel' or 'the Church'?" It is obvious that they were both!

As the early Jewish Church expanded in the book of Acts, these questions were eventually raised: "Is our Messiah only for us? What about the Gentiles?" After the Holy Spirit fell unexpectedly on the Gentiles (Acts

10:44, 45), narrowness and prejudice slowly began to break down. A Jewish council of believers convened in Jerusalem to discuss "the Jew and Gentile" question (Acts chapter 15). Finally, the Holy Spirit broke through the fog and revealed to the apostles what had actually been accomplished by Jesus Christ. A new day had dawned. The wall had come down. It had been demolished by the cross!

A number of years later, Paul wrote to believing Gentiles: "Wherefore remember, that ye being in time past Gentiles in the flesh, who are called Uncircumcision by that which is called the Circumcision in the flesh made by hands; That at that time ye were without Christ, being aliens from the commonwealth of Israel, and strangers from the covenants of promise, having no hope, and without God in the world: But now in Christ Jesus ye who sometimes were far off are made nigh by the blood of Christ. For he is our peace, who hath made both one, and hath broken down the middle wall of partition between us ... to make in himself of twain one new man, so making peace; And that he might reconcile both unto God in one body by the cross." Ephesians 2:11-16. Here Paul is quite clear. Believing "non-Jews" were "in time past Gentiles ... aliens from the commonwealth of Israel." But "now in Christ Jesus," Jews and Gentiles have become "one." It is the *truth*. So let's come out of the fog! The wall came tumbling down at the cross!

Paul was enraptured by this theme. He wrote a lot about it. "Whereby, when ye read, ye may understand my knowledge in the mystery of Christ Which in other ages was not made known unto the sons of men, as it is now revealed unto his holy apostles and prophets by the Spirit; That the Gentiles should be fellow heirs, and of the same body." Ephesians 3:4-6. Here Paul called this uniting of Jews and Gentiles into "the same body" the "mystery of Christ," which is "now" being revealed "by the Spirit." This mystery is more important than any mystery movie you might watch on TV. Again, Paul wrote, "There is neither Jew nor Greek, there is neither bond nor free, there is neither male nor female: for ye are all one in Christ Jesus." Galatians 3:28. As pastors often say during marriage ceremonies, "What God has joined together, let no man separate!" This now applies to Jews and Gentiles in Jesus Christ!

According to the New Testament, believing Jews and believing Gentiles are now one. The two combined are "Abraham's seed." Galatians 3:29. This is now "the Israel of God." Galatians 6:15, 16. This "mystery" has been accomplished through the cross. Jesus Christ did it. When He died, He broke down the wall. Now think about it. Should Christians rebuild a wall that Jesus Christ died to abolish?

Yet what about Paul's statement in Romans 11:26 that "all Israel shall be saved"? Some have applied this to a mass conversion of the Jewish nation at

Armageddon. Yet the context reveals otherwise. When Paul wrote that "all Israel shall be saved," he did not mean that at some point "every Jew would be saved." In the same chapter he wrote, "If by any means I may provoke to emulation them which are my flesh, and might save *some* of them." Verse 14, emphasis added. Again, in the same chapter, Paul declared "And they also, if they abide not still in unbelief, shall be grafted in." Verse 23.

It is true that "all Israel shall be saved." But, as we studied in Chapter 3 of this book, the big question is "Which Israel?" Remember, "they are not all Israel, which are of Israel." Romans 9:6. There is a natural Israel according to the flesh, and there is an Israel in the Spirit made up of Jews and Gentiles who believe in Jesus Christ. To apply the "all Israel" which "shall be saved" to a group of Jews who are separate from the Church is to rebuild the wall which Jesus Christ died to abolish!

Who then is the "all Israel" in Romans 11:26? The answer is in the context. Paul wrote, "I speak to you Gentiles, inasmuch as I am the apostle of the Gentiles, I magnify mine office: If by any means I may provoke to emulation them which are my flesh, and might save some of them." Verse 13, 14. Paul hoped that as the Gentiles responded to his preaching about the Messiah, that this would "provoke ... some" of his Jewish countrymen to re-examine the claims of Christ.

Hopefully, this would lead "some of them to believe in Jesus. Then this combined group of believing Jews and believing Gentiles would form the "all Israel" which shall be saved.

Now for the entire context. "For I would not, brethren, that you should be ignorant of this mystery, lest you should be wise in your own conceits; that blindness in part is happened to Israel, until the fullness of the Gentiles be come in. And so all Israel shall be saved: as it is written, There shall come out of Sion the Deliverer, and shall turn away ungodliness from Jacob: For this is my covenant unto them, when I shall take away their sins." Verses 25-27. The context clearly reveals that the "all Israel" in verse 26 is a united group of believing Jews and believing Gentiles who have responded to the gospel. To believe otherwise is to deny the context, reject "the mystery," and to rebuild the wall that Jesus Christ died to abolish.

God Almighty told Moses on Mount Sinai that "if" the Israelites obeyed His voice, "then" they would be "a peculiar treasure... a kingdom of priests, and an holy nation." Exodus 19:5, 6. In his first letter to believers, Peter used these same words that God had spoken to Israel, and he applied them to the Church. "But *ye* are a chosen generation, a royal priesthood, and holy nation, a peculiar people... Which in time past were not a people, but are now the people of God." 1 Peter 2:9, 10, emphasis added.

In the Old Testament, God spoke about "Israel mine elect." Isaiah 45:4. In the New Testament, Paul wrote "to the saints and faithful brethren in Christ" in Colosse (Colossians 1:2). After reminding them that there is now "neither Greek nor Jew," Paul then specifically told the believers that they were "the elect of God." Colossians 3:11,12.

Thus Peter and Paul agreed. They both took the exact words that God spoke in the Old Testament about Israel and applied them to Jews and Gentiles who believe in Jesus Christ! They both taught that believing Jews and Gentiles, combined, "are now the people of God" (1 Peter 2:9,10; Colossians 3:11, 12; Galatians 6:16). The "two" are now "one" and are of "of the same body." Ephesians 2:14-16; 3:6. Through His cross, Jesus Christ Himself has performed this mysterious wedding ceremony. Therefore, what God has joined together, let no man seperate!

Heavy fog on a highway can be dangerous. It often results in fatal car wrecks. As we shall soon see, if we do not come out of the fog of falsehood about Jews and Gentiles, we just might crash at Armageddon!

CHAPTER 8

1948 — AN "UNSINKABLE" DOCTRINE?

When the horrors of World War II were finally over and Adolf Hitler's Third Reich had come to an end, the world awoke to the full result of the German dictator's "Final Solution." Approximately six million innocent Jews had been brutally murdered. Public opinion then favored the return of the Jews to their ancient homeland.

The British controlled Palestine until May of 1948. On May 14, by resolution of the General Assembly of the United Nations, the Jewish Zionist Movement proclaimed the rebirth of the State of Israel. For almost 2,000 years the Jewish people had been "wanderers among the nations." Now they were home. Yet their struggles had just begun.

An Arab League composed of Egyptians, Iraqis, Syrians, and Jordanians quickly invaded Palestine in an attempt to crush out the new nation. The fighting was heavy. Yet by 1949 the Arabs were defeated, and Israel was still in the land. In May of 1967, Egypt, Jordan, and Syria prepared for another attack. The Israelis struck first, and the war was over in six days. In 1973, at the beginning of the Jewish season of Yom Kippur, the Egyptians and Syrians attacked again. The battles were fierce and bloody. Yet by 1974, Israel was again on top and still in the land.

For more than 50 years these astonishing events have gripped the attention of much of the Christian world. A conclusion has been reached by millions. This must be the fulfillment of Bible prophecy. Today this conviction is being expressed all over planet Earth. The rebirth of the State of Israel in 1948 is now considered by countless Christians to be the most significant prophetic event of the 20th century!

An example of this conviction may be found in the popular book *The Next 7 Great Events of the Future.* Author Randal Ross declares: "I call the establishment of the State of Israel 'the ultimate prophecy time bomb,' because when Israel became a legitimate state in the eyes of the world in May 1948, that single, seemingly isolated incident started the prophetic timeclock ticking down toward the 'zero hour' and the end of time."[1] Hal Lindsey echoed, "Since the restoration of Israel as a nation in 1948, we have lived in the most significant period of prophetic history."[2]   It is not an understatement to say that the vast majority of current Christian beliefs about the end-times rest firmly upon this 1948 platform.

On April 10, 1912, the Titanic set sail from England for America. The largest ship in the world at that time, she was considered to be unsinkable. Then, after four days of smooth sailing, she hit the ice. Three hours later she was under water, on her way down to the bottom of the Atlantic Ocean. In many ways, the 1948 theory is like the Titanic. In the minds of countless Christians, it is considered to be unsinkable. However, in a few moments, this popular theory is going to hit the ice of God's Word. If it begins to sink, then we should abandon ship as soon as possible!

There are three main arguments now being used to support the theory that Bible prophecy was fulfilled in 1948. It is time to carefully examine these arguments.

1. The "Fig Tree" Argument

Hal Lindsey wrote: "Jesus predicts an extremely important time clue. He says, 'Now learn a parable of the fig tree' [Matthew 24:32, 33 quoted]. ... The most important sign in Matthew has to be the restoration of the Jews to the land in the rebirth of Israel. ... When the Jewish people ... became a nation again on 14 May 1948 the 'fig tree' put forth its first leaves. Jesus said that this would indicate that He was 'at the door,' ready to return."[3]

Is this really what Jesus said? In a parallel passage, Luke records: "And he spake to them a parable; Behold the fig tree, and all the trees; When they now shoot forth, ye see and know of your own selves that summer is now nigh at hand. So likewise ye, when ye see these things come to pass, know ye that the kingdom of God is nigh at hand." Luke 21:29-31.

Because Luke wrote, "and all the trees; when they now shoot forth," we can clearly see that Jesus did not have in mind just one tree representing Israel in 1948. In Matthew, Jesus explained His parable of the fig tree. He said, "So likewise ye, when ye shall see all these things, know that it is near, even at the doors." Matthew 24:34. When fig trees, and all trees, start blooming at the end of winter, we know that summer is near. "So likewise," said Jesus, when we see "all these" various signs given in Matthew chapter 24 occurring at the same time, then we may know that His return is near. The fig tree is not the sign. It simply represents "all" the signs in Matthew chapter 24, none of which is the specified rebirth of Israel in 1948. The ice of God's Word has just ripped the first hole in the bottom of the 1948 ship!

2. The "Israeli Victories" Argument
The idea is often expressed that the Israeli victories over the Arabs in 1949, 1967, and 1973 is strong

evidence that God had regathered Israel and was now fighting in behalf of His chosen nation, even though the leadership of that nation still does not believe in Jesus Christ. Again, let's examine the argument.

First of all, the Bible says that Jesus Christ is the same yesterday, today, and forever (Hebrews 13:8). God says, "I am the Lord, I change not." Malachi 3:6. Let's examine the Scriptures with this principle in mind. Was God able to fight for Israel in the Old Testament when they were in unbelief?

After the Exodus, God promised to bring Israel into the Promised Land (Exodus 33:1-3). Twelve men were sent in to spy out the territory. Yet after all the people heard the "evil report" about "the giants" in the land, they "murmured against Moses," saying, "let us return into Egypt" (Numbers 13:32, 33; 14:2, 4). Then God Himself pronounced this judgment: "But as for you, your carcasses, they shall fall in the wilderness. And your children shall wander in the wilderness forty years. ... And ye shall know my breach of promise." Numbers 14:32, 34. Thus, because of Israel's unbelief, God was unable to fulfill His promise to that generation.

Sadly, the ancient Israelites were unwilling to accept that 40-year sentence. The people then proposed to go up anyway "unto the place which the Lord hath promised." Numbers 14:40. But Moses said, "It shall not prosper. Go not up, for the Lord is not among you.

... Therefore the Lord will not be with you. ... But they presumed to go up. ... Then the Amalekites came down ... and smote them." Numbers 14:42-45. This passage is full of instruction. Because of Israel's unbelief, God could not fight for them. Years later, when Israel again "forsook the Lord ... they could not any longer stand before their enemies." Judges 2:13, 14. This basic Bible truth is repeated many times in Joshua, Judges, Samuel, Kings, Chronicles, Jeremiah, etc.

God does not change. All throughout sacred history, He could not fight for Israel while they were in unbelief. Thus He could not have been fighting for the Jewish nation in 1949, 1967, and 1973! Just because a nation wins battles, this is not evidence in itself that God is fighting for that nation. Was God fighting for Hitler when he won so many battles? Was the Lord on the side of the Nazis when they cruelly murdered six million Jews? Obviously not! Dear friend, the "Israeli Victory" argument is not based on a thorough study of the Word of God. Ice has just ripped hole number two in the hull of this "unsinkable" theory!

3. The End-Time Regathering Argument

This is "the big one." The idea is now being expressed all over the world that ancient prophecies found in the Old Testament, which predict a regathering of Israel back into their land, were fulfilled in 1948. The main prophecy used to support this conclusion is found in Ezekiel chapters 36-38.

In *The Late Great Planet Earth,* Hal Lindsey gives the following three reasons why Ezekiel's prophecy must point to a 1948 fulfillment: (1) God said concerning Israel: "I will take you from among the heathen, and gather you out of all countries, and bring you into your own land." Ezekiel 36:24. (2) The phrase "out of all countries," applies to a "world wide dispersion," and therefore cannot apply to the time of the Babylonian captivity. (3) Ezekiel's prophecy will be fulfilled "in the latter days" (38:16), which, according to Hal Lindsey, is a "definite" term applying to "the time just preceding" the second coming of Jesus Christ.[4] These three reasons have been accepted by countless Christians as "unsinkable" evidence in favor of a 1948 fulfillment.

The following five arguments not only cast doubt upon the three points just listed, but also prove that Bible prophecy could not have been fulfilled in 1948!

1. God specifically told ancient Israel that He would gather them "from all the nations" *immediately* "after seventy years be accomplished at Babylon." Jeremiah 29:10, 14, 18.

2. The time period right after the Babylonian captivity is also called "the latter days" (Jeremiah 29:10-14; 30:24; 27:2-7; 48:47; 49:39; 50:1). Thus, the

phrase "the latter days" is not always a "definite term" that applies to "the time just preceding" the second coming of Jesus. Moses told ancient Israel, "I know that after my death ... evil will befall you in the latter days." Deuteronomy 31:29.

3. Three times in Ezekiel chapter 38, the regathered Israelites are described as a people who "dwell safely all of them" (verse 8), "are at rest, that dwell safely, all of them dwelling without walls" (verse 11), and "my people of Israel dwelleth safely" (verse 14)." These words definitely do not apply to modern Israelis, who now "dwell" in the midst of terrorism, Arab hostility, bomb threats, and the plots of the PLO.

4. The reason why the Israelites were scattered in the Old Testament was because they forsook God, broke His law, and disobeyed His word (Jeremiah 16:10-13; 29:18, 19). If you search carefully, you will discover that, according to the Bible, Israel must first repent of her sins *before* such a regathering can be accomplished by God.

Here is the proof. God said to Israel: "It shall come to pass, when all these things are come upon thee, the blessing and the curse ... and thou shalt call them to mind among all the nations, whither the Lord thy God hath driven thee, And shalt *return* unto the Lord thy God, and shalt *obey* his voice ... *then* the Lord thy God will turn thy captivity ... and will return and gather thee from all the nations." Deuteronomy 30:1-3, emphasis added.

According to these inspired words, when God scatters Israel among "all the nations," if they *return* and *obey* His voice, *then* He will regather them. If they do not return and obey, then this prophecy cannot be fulfilled by God! Because the Messiah has come, this "return to the Lord" must be a return to Jesus Christ. It is clear that Jewish Zionism did not meet this spiritual condition in 1948.

Again, God told ancient Israel, "If ye transgress, I will scatter you abroad among the nations: But if ye turn to me ... yet will I gather them." Nehemiah 1:8, 9. "And ye shall seek me, and find me, *when* ye shall search for me with all your heart. And I will be found of you, saith the Lord: and I will turn away your captivity, and I will gather you from all the nations." Jeremiah 29:13, 14, emphasis added. These Scriptures are very plain. Israel must first repent, *then* God will gather her. Once again, this condition was not met by the Zionist movement in 1948. The "unsinkable" theory is starting to go down. "Lower the lifeboats" is the cry from heaven!

The most important "regathering prophecy" found in Ezekiel chapter 36 also contains the conditional elements taught in Scripture. Notice carefully, "Thus saith the Lord God. *In the day* that I shall have cleansed you from *all* your iniquities *I will also cause* you to dwell in the cities, and the wastes shall be builded." Ezekiel 36:33, emphasis added. Thus, "in the day" that God cleanses Israel from "all" her sins, in that day He would "also cause" her to dwell in her cities. This did not happen in 1948! Israel as a nation was not cleansed from "all" her iniquities at that time. It had not confessed and forsaken its past sin of rejecting the Son (Matthew 21:37-39).

Jonah predicted, "Yet forty days, and Nineveh shall be overthrown." Jonah 3:4. Yet 40 days later, Nineveh was not overthrown. Why? Because the prophecy was conditional. Nineveh repented, so God's judgment was deferred. As we have seen, the same conditional elements are also found in the regathering prophecies. Because Israel did not first repent and return to the Lord Jesus Christ, the promises of regathering could not have been fulfilled by God in 1948.

5. The prophet Ezekiel declared: "And the word of the Lord came unto me, saying, Son of man, set thy face against Gog, the land of Magog." "In the latter years thou shalt come into the land that is brought back from the sword, and is gathered out of many people." "Thou shalt ascend and come" "upon the people that are gathered out of the nations." "And it shall come to pass at the same time when Gog shall come against the land of Israel, saith the Lord God, that my fury shall

come up in my face." "I will rain upon him, and upon his bands, and upon the many people that are with him, an overflowing rain, and great hailstones, fire, and brimstone. ... And they shall know that I am the Lord." Ezekiel 38:1, 2, 8, 9, 12, 18, 22, 23.

Chapter 5 of *The Late Great Planet Earth* is called "Russia Is a Gog." There Hal Lindsey applied the words of Ezekiel chapter 38 to the restoration of Israel in 1948 and then to a final Middle East battle between Russia and the Jewish nation. Yet the explosive truth is that the book of Revelation actually applies Ezekiel's prophecy to a global event that will occur at the end of the millennium.

In Chapter 2 of this book we discovered how Matthew took Hosea 11:1, which originally applied to the nation of Israel, and then declared it "fulfilled" in Jesus Christ (Matthew 2:15). We also saw how Paul made a similar "Old Testament to New Testament application" when he applied "the seed of Abraham," which was definitely "Israel," to "one ... which is Christ" (Isaiah 41:8; Galatians 3:16). Fasten your seatbelts! The book of Revelation does the same thing with Ezekiel chapter 38!

Revelation 20:7-9 says: "And when the thousand years are expired, Satan shall be loosed out of his prison, And shall go out to deceive the nations which are in the four quarters of the earth, Gog and Magog, to gather them together to battle: the number of whom is as the sand of the sea. And they went up on the breadth of the earth, and compassed the camp of the saints about, and the beloved city: and fire came down from God out of heaven, and devoured them."

The major elements are the same. Both Ezekiel chapter 38 and Revelation chapter 20 speak about Gog, Magog, a great army, a final gathering for battle against Jerusalem, and fire from heaven. Yet Revelation chapter 20 applies these things to the end of the millennium, to a global Gog and Magog, and to a final global battle against the camp of the saints and the beloved city, which is the new Jerusalem (Revelation 3:12; 21:10; Hebrews 12:22). Thus Revelation chapter 20 takes what originally applied to the literal Jewish nation and then applies it to a final global battle against the saints of Jesus Christ, who are inside the new Jerusalem at the end of the millennium.

Why does Revelation do this? For the same reason we discussed in Chapter 3 of this book. So that the "word of God" will not be made of "none effect" through the unbelief of many natural Jews. (See Romans 9:6.) God did promise in Ezekiel chapter 38 (and in Zechariah chapter 14) that He would defend Israel and Jerusalem during a final battle. And He will. He will defend His Israel in the Spirit, which will dwell inside the new Jerusalem at the end of the millennium!

According to Revelation 20:7-9, this is how Ezekiel chapter 38 will be fulfilled. Therefore, the big question is "Are we willing to accept the New Testament's application of Old Testament prophecies?" If not, then we are not being faithful to the entire Word of God!

On April 15, 1912, at 2:20 a.m., the unsinkable Titanic was fully underwater. About a third of her passengers were in lifeboats, while the majority were on their way to the bottom of the Atlantic Ocean. How about us? Will we abandon the "1948 Ship" before it is too late? Our Captain is now pleading, "Get into the lifeboats!" If we refuse, we may go down to the bottom of the sea!

[1]Randal Ross, *The Next 7 Great Events of the Future*, (Lake Mary, Fla.: Creation House), © 1979, p. 23.

[2]Hal Lindsey with C.C. Carlson, *The Late Great Planet Earth* (Grand Rapids, Mich.: Zondervan), 1970, p. 51.

[3]*Ibid.,* p. 43.

[4]*Ibid.,* pp. 49, 50.

CHAPTER 9

TITANIC TRUTHS ABOUT THE TEMPLE

On April 15, 1912, the Titanic sank to the bottom of the Atlantic Ocean. There it remained, undiscovered for decades. In 1980, a rich Texas oilman decided to fund a search for the lost ship. Two expeditions went out to sea, yet they found nothing. In 1985, another group of researchers set sail from France. They pinpointed a 12-mile area in which they thought the ship had rested. After two months of deep-sea surveying, their sophisticated ocean-scanning devices located a large object on the sea floor. As the outlines of a ship became clearer, the shout finally rang out: "This is it! We have found the Titanic!" The discovery was reported in newspapers around the world.

In this chapter, we will continue to survey the hidden depths of the Word of God. We do not need any sophisticated equipment, though—only open hearts. As we set sail into the following paragraphs, we will discover things more shocking than what those researchers uncovered in 1985. Are you ready? It is now time to discover Titanic truths about the temple!

It is a fact that several Jewish organizations in Jerusalem are now preparing for the rebuilding of a third Jewish temple on the Temple Mount. A popular Christian book called *The Edge of Time,* by Peter and Patti Lalonde, gives the following report: "A model of the Third Temple has been constructed and sits on exhibit in old Jerusalem. Even a computerized list of candidates who fulfill the requirements of a Temple priest has been drawn up, and rabbinical students have been training for ancient Jewish temple rites and sacrifice."[1] Many religious Jews want another Temple. Millions of Christians now believe the Bible definitely predicts one will be built. *But does it really?* Is it possible that the "third temple" theory is yet another grand delusion of the last days?

First of all, let's focus on what happened before the second temple was destroyed. When Jesus Christ died, "the veil of the temple was rent in twain from the top to the bottom; and the earth did quake." Matthew 27:51. By ripping the veil, God Almighty showed all mankind that the value of animal sacrifices was over. The earthly temple service was coming to an end. Why? Because the great Sacrifice had just been offered! A few years later, Paul wrote in reference to the earthly temple, "Now that which decayeth and waxeth old is ready to vanish away." Hebrews 8:13. In A.D. 70, the second temple was demolished by the Romans.

Now think for a moment. Would the providence of God ever lead the Jewish people to rebuild a third temple? Would the Father ever initiate the restarting of sacrifices that ended with the death of His Son? When Jesus cried out, "It is finished" (John 19:30), He abolished all sacrifices. He was the final Sacrifice! Therefore, would not the restarting of sacrifices be an open denial that Jesus Christ is the Messiah? If Israel ever did rebuild a third temple and begin to offer sacrifices, would not this be another official, national rejection of the Saviour? What happened 2,000 years ago when the leaders of Israel officially rejected their Messiah? The result was disaster! More than a million Jews perished.

Three main sections of Scripture are being used today by Christians to support the "third temple" theory. They are Daniel 9:27, assorted "temple texts" in the book of Revelation, and 2 Thessalonians 2:4. Yet in all three of these sections, nothing is said about any temple being "rebuilt." In the Old Testament, major portions of Scripture are devoted to the building of the wilderness tabernacle, the first temple, and the second temple (Exodus chapters 35-40; 1 Kings chapter 6; Ezra chapters 3-6). Yet concerning the *literal rebuilding* of a third Jewish temple, we find nothing.

Argument 1—The use of Daniel 9:27

Popular prophecy scholars today argue that when Daniel 9:27 describes the coming of one who will "cause the sacrifice ... to cease," this must refer to an end-time Antichrist who will stop the sacrifices of a rebuilt Jewish temple. Yet we proved in Chapter 5 of this book that it was Jesus Christ who already caused "the sacrifice ... to cease" 2,000 years ago through His death on the cross. Matthew Henry faithfully declared that it was Jesus who would "cause the sacrifice and oblation to cease. By offering himself a sacrifice once and for all he shall put an end to all the Levitical sacrifices."[2] Therefore, when people use Daniel 9:27 as a foundation text to support the idea of a "rebuilt third temple," they are actually trying to build a house on sand. Worse yet. They are building on top of a major earthquake fault line!

Argument 2—"Temple texts" in the book of Revelation

These texts all concern the heavenly temple, not a rebuilt third temple on earth. Revelation 11:19 says, "The temple of God was opened in heaven." Revelation 14:17 says that "another angel came out of the temple which is in heaven." Revelation 15:5 declares that "the temple ... in heaven was opened," and Revelation 16:17 says, "There came a great voice out of the temple of heaven." Thus there is a temple in heaven. And it is in this temple that Jesus Christ, our Great High Priest, now ministers His blood in our behalf (Hebrews 8:1, 2; 9:12, 14). It is also to this temple that Paul counsels Christians to look (Hebrews 10:19-22). We will study this subject more thoroughly in Chapter 12 of this book.

Argument 3—The use of 2 Thessalonians 2:4

This is probably the most important passage used to support the "third temple" theory. Here Paul wrote that the Antichrist would sit "in the temple of God, shewing himself that he is God." 2 Thessalonians 2:4. Hal Lindsey comments: "It is certain that the Temple will be rebuilt. Prophecy demands it. ... "[The Antichrist] takes his seat in the temple of God, displaying himself as being God" (2 Thessalonians 2:4). ... We must conclude that a third Temple will be rebuilt upon its ancient site in old Jerusalem."[3]

2 Thessalonians 2:1-8 is one of the most controversial passages in the Bible. It is time to examine this section carefully. In this analysis, I will draw on the past insights of historic Protestants, which was commonly accepted doctrine in Europe, England, and America for over 300 years—since the time of the Reformation.

An Analysis of 2 Thessalonians 2:1-8

Verse 1—"Now we beseech you, brethren, by the coming of our Lord Jesus Christ, and by our gathering together unto him." Jesus is "coming" to gather His children. The Greek word used here for "coming" is *parousia,* which clearly refers to the second coming of Jesus Christ (Matthew 24:27).

Verse 2—"That ye be not soon shaken in mind, or be troubled, neither by spirit, nor by word, nor by letter as from us, as that the day of Christ is at hand." Here Paul warned the Thessalonians not to be troubled by anyone who would suggest that "the day of Christ" on which He would "gather" His children was "at hand" in the first century. No. Something big must happen first.

Verse 3—"Let no man deceive you by any means: for that day [when Jesus comes to gather His children] shall not come, except there come a falling away first, and that man of sin [Antichrist] be revealed, the son of perdition." Here Paul is very clear. "That day" when Jesus comes to "gather" us shall not come until there is first "a falling away" and the Antichrist is revealed! Thus, contrary to popular opinion, Antichrist comes *before* Jesus comes to gather His people! Paul warned, "Let no man deceive you by any means" into believing anything else.

The phrase, "a falling away," is from the Greek word "apostasia," which means "a falling away" from the truth. Thus, there would be in the history of Christianity, as in the history of Israel, a major "falling away" from God's Word that would result in the rise of Antichrist. Paul called this Antichrist "that man of sin." These words actually point to an earlier prophecy found in Daniel chapter 7.

Daniel chapter 7 predicted the rise of a "little horn" with "eyes like the eyes of a man." Daniel 7:8. Daniel did not say the little horn would be a man, but that it would have "eyes like the eyes of a man." This horn would arise out of "the fourth beast," or "fourth kingdom" (verse 23), which was the Roman Empire. It would arise "among" the 10 horns in Europe (verse 8), would speak proud words against God (verses 8, 25) and would make "war with the saints" (verse 21) in Christian history.

Paul also called the Antichrist "the son of perdition," which is what Jesus Christ called Judas (John 17:12). Judas was an insider, an apostle, one of the twelve. Judas kissed Jesus, calling him "Master" (Mark 14:45). Yet it was a kiss of betrayal. By calling Antichrist "the son of perdition," Paul gives us a clue in that this deceiver would not be a pagan dictator like Adolf Hitler, but rather a professed apostle of Jesus Christ. Yet in reality, he would be a false apostle. (See 2 Corinthians 11:13.)

Verse 4—"Who opposeth and exalteth himself above all that is called God, or is worshipped; so that he as God sitteth in the temple of God, shewing himself that he is God." Paul did not say, as so many believe, that Antichrist will walk into a temple and say, "I am

God." Rather, he would sit "as God ... shewing himself that he is God." The difference is subtle, yet very important. The Antichrist will not "say it," for this would be too obvious. Yet he will "show it" by his actions.

The Antichrist will "sit." This does not mean he will "sit down" on some chair. In the language of the Bible, to "sit" means to sit in a position of authority. Jesus Christ now "sits" at the right hand of God (Mark 16:19). He is our supreme authority, the only Mediator between God and men (1 Timothy 2:5). According to Paul, the Antichrist will also deceptively "sit" in a position of authority. Yet this "sitting" will actually be in opposition to the supreme authority of Jesus Christ!

Antichrist will even "sit in the temple of God." Here is the key text! Millions of sincere Christians, like Hal Lindsey, apply this to a rebuilt third Jewish temple in Jerusalem. But is that right? Think about it. Let's say that a group of Jewish people, who do not believe in the great sacrifice of Jesus Christ, were to rebuild a third temple on the Temple Mount. Could that temple ever really be called "the temple of God"? No! For that temple would be in itself a denial of Jesus Christ! Notice what the famous Christian commentator Adam Clarke had to say about Paul's words: "By the temple of God the apostle could not well mean the temple of Jerusalem; because that, he knew, would be destroyed within a few years. After the death of Christ the temple of Jerusalem is never called by the apostles *the temple of God.*"[4]

The Greek word Paul used here for "temple" is "naos." One Titanic truth about the temple is that every time Paul used the word "naos" in his letters, he always applied it *not* to a building in Jerusalem, but to the Church! Paul wrote to "the church of God which is at Corinth," saying, "Know ye not that ye are the temple ["naos"] of God?" 1 Corinthians 1:2; 3:16. (See also 2 Corinthians 6:16; Ephesians 2:19-22.) Thus, to Paul, "the temple of God" is the Christian Church! Again, Adam Clarke commented: "Under the gospel dispensation, the *temple of God* is the Church of Christ."[5] And this is where Antichrist will sit! He will deceptively enter the Church, like Judas, who was one of the twelve! Then he will "sit" in a position of supreme, apparently infallible authority, which will ever so subtly counterfeit the supreme authority of Jesus Christ!

If you were the devil, wouldn't you try to do the same thing? You wouldn't spend most of your time hanging out in a bar. Your goal would be to try and deceive Christians! If you were Satan, wouldn't you want to sneak into the Church, get behind the pulpit, and then preach a sermon? (See Acts 20:28-31; 1 Timothy 4:1; 2 Timothy 4:3, 4.) This is exactly what Paul says the Antichrist will do! He will cleverly enter the temple of God, which is the Christian Church, and then he will "sit" in a position of apparently supreme authority as he makes pronouncements on matters of Christian doctrine.

The world-famous Matthew Henry, whose roots were firmly planted in historic Protestantism, commented: "[Paul] speaks of some very great apostasy. ... No sooner was Christianity planted and rooted in the world than there began to be a defection in the Christian church. ... He is called the man of sin, ... the son of perdition. ... These names may properly be applied, for these reasons, to the papal state. ... The bishops of Rome not only oppose God's authority, ... but have exalted themselves above God. ... The antichrist here mentioned is some usurper of God's authority in the Christian church, ... and to whom can this better apply that to the bishops of Rome?"[6]

The above view was shared by John Wycliffe, William Tyndale, Martin Luther, John Calvin, the translators of the King James Bible, John Wesley, Sir Isaac Newton, Charles Spurgeon, Bishop J.C. Ryle, Dr. Martyn Lloyd-Jones, and countless other Protestant reformers. Have we not just discovered a Titanic truth?

Verses 5, 6—"Remember ye not, that, when I was yet with you, I told you these things? And now ye know what witholdeth [restrains] that he might be revealed in his time." This is a very controversial sentence. Multitudes of prophecy scholars today believe that the Holy Spirit inside the Christian church is the restrainer.

They teach that when the Church is removed at the rapture, then the Antichrist will appear. They also teach that after this Antichrist shows up, he will then enter the rebuilt Jewish temple in Jerusalem and proclaim that he is God. This will supposedly happen during "the seven years of tribulation." Yet from what we have studied so far, can you not see that there is something wrong with this picture?

Paul did not specify in this letter "what" was restraining Antichrist. Yet the Thessalonians knew, for Paul said in verse 6 that he had previously "told" them. A study of the writings of the early Church fathers, who were Christian leaders living after the apostles, reveals exactly what the early church believed. "The early Church—from whom *alone* we can learn what Paul told them by word of mouth, but refrained from committing to writing—has left it on record that the Apostle had told them that this hindering power was the dominion of the Roman Caesars; that while they continued to reign at Rome, the development of the predicted power of evil was impossible. ... While the Caesars reigned he [the Antichrist] could not appear, but when they passed away he would succeed them."[7]

Based on historical research, Matthew Henry agreed. "This is supposed [believed] to be the power of the Roman empire, which the apostle did not think fit to mention more plainly at that time; and it is notorious that, while this power continued, it prevented the advances of the bishops of Rome to that height of tyranny to which soon afterwards they arrived."[8] Thus, the force that "witholdeth," or restrains, was the imperial power of the Roman Empire ruled by the Caesars. It was only after Rome fell, in A.D. 476, that the popes were free to rule. This used to be a common interpretation among Lutheran, Baptist, Presbyterian, and Methodist scholars for 300 years after the Reformation. But times have changed. New scholars are here with new ideas.

Verse 7—"For the mystery of iniquity doth already work: only he who now letteth [restrains] will let, until he be taken out of the way." In Paul's day, because of the restraining power of the Roman empire, the Antichrist's rise to power was being hindered. Yet Daniel's previous prophecy predicted the eventual fall of the fourth beast (the Roman Empire), which would then allow the "little horn" (Antichrist) to fully spring into action (Daniel 7:7, 8). In his epistle to the Thessalonians, Paul did not specify in writing that the Roman Empire would eventually be "taken out of the way." The reason was because his letter might be discovered by Roman authorities, which might have resulted in more "persecutions and tribulations" against his converts for their perceived disloyalty to Caesar. (See 2 Thessalonians 1:4.) This view fits with prophecy and history. Not only that, it makes perfect sense!

In Paul's day, the "mystery of iniquity" was already working. Yet it was largely hidden. It was not until the Roman Empire finally fell in A.D. 476 that this "mystery" was fully revealed for what it was to the eyes of the world. Then came the Dark Ages, when Europe was held in a grip of terror for almost 1,000 years. Historians estimate that the "Holy Office of the Inquisition" was responsible for the brutal torture and deaths of 50-100 million Christians. And this was done in the name of Jesus Christ! Surely Antichrist has entered the temple of God.

Verse 8—"And then shall that Wicked be revealed, whom the Lord shall consume with the spirit of his mouth, and shall destroy with the brightness of his coming." Thus "the mystery of iniquity" would start in the days of Paul and would continue to the end. Then it will be destroyed by the "brightness of his coming." The Greek word for "coming" used in verse 8 is the same word for "coming" used in verse 1. That word is *parousia,* which clearly refers to the second coming of Jesus Christ. Thus, according to verses 1 and 8, it is at the second coming, *after* Antichrist is revealed, that Jesus Christ will come to "gather" His children.

A SIMPLE SUMMARY OF 2 THESSALONIANS 2:1-8

Verse 1—Jesus Christ is "coming" [the *parousia*] to "gather" His children.

Verse 2—Paul told the early Thessalonian believers not be "shaken" by false ideas that this "day of Christ" was "at hand" in the first century.

Verse 3—Before "the day of Christ" comes, "a falling away" must come *first*, then the prophesied "man of sin" would be revealed.

Verse 4—This "man of sin" will exalt himself and will even sit in "the temple of God," *which is the Church*, "shewing himself that he is God."

Verse 5—Paul had previously warned the Thessalonians about this.

Verse 6—The Thessalonians knew "what" was then restraining the Antichrist.

Verse 7—The Antichrist was already working secretly in the first century. Soon the restraining power would be "taken out of the way."

Verse 8—Then the Antichrist would be fully "revealed." *After* his revelation, he would continue until the second coming of Jesus. Then he will be "destroyed" by the "brightness" of Christ's "coming" [the *parousia*]. And it is at this second coming, at the *parousia, after* the Antichrist is revealed, that Jesus Christ will "gather" His children who have remained faithful to the truth!

So what have we discovered in the deep waters of the Bible? Something much bigger than what those researchers uncovered in 1985. We have discovered Titanic truths about the temple! We have learned that there is nothing in Scripture about the rebuilding of a third Jewish temple on the Temple Mount! When Revelation speaks of a temple, it is always referring to "the temple of heaven." Revelation 16:17. And when Paul wrote about the Antichrist entering the temple of God, he was talking about his entrance into the Church! If certain people who reject the final sacrifice of Jesus Christ ever do rebuild a third temple on the Temple Mount inside Jerusalem, it definitely will not be "the temple of God"!

So don't be fooled. Millions today are expecting some tricky Antichrist to show up after all the Christians are raptured away from this world. Books that teach this are best sellers. Videos that promote this are eagerly watched all over America. Few seriously question these ideas. Even less are looking for deception to occur *inside* the Church! Yet Paul was writing to us when he warned, "Let no man deceive *you* by any means." 2 Thessalonians 2:3, emphasis added. That word "you" means *you and me*! May God help us to stay close to Jesus Christ and to avoid the deceptions of those who have "fallen away" from the truth.

---

[1]Peter and Patti Lalonde, *The Edge of Time*, p. 41.

[2]*Matthew Henry's Commentary on the Whole Bible*, Vol. IV—Isaiah to Malachi, Complete Edition (New York: Fleming H. Revell Co.) 1712, notes on Daniel 9:27, p. 1095.

[3]Hal Lindsey with C.C. Carlson, *The Late Great Planet Earth*, (Grand Rapids, Mich.: Zondervan), 1970, pp. 45, 46.

[4]*The New Testament of Our Lord and Saviour Jesus Christ*, with a commentary and critical notes by Adam Clarke, Vol. 11—Romans to the Revelations (New York: Abingdon-Cokesbury Press), notes on 2 Thessalonians 2:3, 4, p. 602.

[5]*Ibid.*

[6]*Matthew Henry's Commentary on the Whole Bible*, Vol. VI—Acts to Revelation, Complete Edition (New York: Fleming H. Revell Co.), notes on 2 Thessalonians 2:3, 4, p. 798.

[7]H. Grattan Guiness, *Romanism and the Reformation* (Rapidan, Va.: Hartland Publications), © 1995 (originally published in 1887), p. 51.

[8]*Matthew Henry's Commentary on the Whole Bible*, Vol. VI—Acts to Revelation, Complete Edition (New York: Fleming H. Revell Co.), notes on 2 Thessalonians 2:5-7, p. 798.

CHAPTER 10

WHEN THE RIVER EUPHRATES RUNS DRY

We have reached the heart of this book. It is finally time to study the book of Revelation. As we open its sacred pages, we discover statements about mount Sion (14:1), the twelve tribes of Israel (7:4-8), Jerusalem (21:10), the temple (11:19), Sodom and Egypt (11:8), Babylon (17:5), Gog and Magog (20:8), the Euphrates river (16:12), and Armageddon (16:16). Thus, it is obvious that Revelation uses the terminology and geography of the Middle East in its prophecies. Yet what is happening right now all over planet Earth is that sincere evangelical scholars are applying most of these terms literally—to those literal places, and to the Jewish nation in the Middle East. Once again, here is the "highly explosive" question: Does God want these prophecies to be applied to the Israel in the flesh, or to His Israel in the Spirit?

One example of such Middle East literalism is the following interpretation of Revelation 16:12. The Bible says, "The sixth angel poured out his vial upon the great river Euphrates; and the water thereof was dried up, that the way of the kings of the east might be prepared." Revelation 16:12. A popular Christian magazine called *Endtime* comments: "EUPHRATES RIVER TO BE DRIED UP: In Revelation 16:12, the Bible predicts that the Euphrates River will be dried up to prepare the way for the kings of the east to invade Israel. This will happen at the time of the battle of Armageddon. ... On January 13th, 1990, the *Indianapolis Star* carried the headline 'Turkey will cut off flow of Euphrates for 1 month.' The article stated that a huge reservoir had been built by Turkey. While filling up the reservoir, the flow of the Euphrates would be stopped for one month and a concrete plug for a diversion channel built. These things have now been done. With this newly built dam, Turkey has the ability to stop the Euphrates River at will. The conditions for fulfilling this 1900-year-old prophecy are now in place!"[1]

When many Christians read about the Euphrates drying up, the apply this literally. The kings of the east are often assumed to be China. When modern Turkey built a dam on the Euphrates river, many concluded that soon a massive Chinese army would be able to cross a dry river bed in order to attack Israel at Armageddon. This is supposedly how Revelation 16:12 will be fulfilled. Yet we cannot help but wonder, why would the Chinese ever launch such an army? And if they ever did attack Israel, why would they worry about crossing this river? Why not just send planes and drop bombs? Hasn't the Persian Gulf War taught us that ground armies don't accomplish much in this high-tech age of ours?

We are about to learn from the Bible that such Middle East literalism actually fails to understand the true meaning and genius of the book of Revelation. It fails to discern that Revelation is simply using Old Testament terms, history, and geography as symbols that are then meant to be applied spiritually and globally at the end of time! On August 9, 1945, the United States government finally decided to drop an atomic bomb called the "Fat Man" upon Nagasaki. It is now time to drop our version of the "Fat Man" upon the popular Middle East method of interpreting Bible prophecy.

"The sixth angel poured out his vial upon the great river Euphrates; and the water was dried up, that the way of the kings of the east might be prepared." Revelation 16:12. In order to correctly understand this prophecy, we must first study some ancient Bible history about Israel and Babylon. In 605 B.C., "Nebuchadnezzar king of Babylon" came "unto Jerusalem, and besieged it." Daniel 1:1. Jerusalem was conquered and Israel was taken captive for 70 years (Daniel 9:2). After those 70 years, an amazing set of circumstances occurred. The Euphrates was dried up, Babylon was conquered from the east, and Israel was delivered. As we shall soon see, this history forms the background for a *true* understanding of Revelation 16:12.

Ancient Babylon sat on the river Euphrates (Jeremiah 51:63, 64). A wall surrounded the city. The river Euphrates ran through Babylon, entering and exiting through two spiked gates whose bars reached down to the riverbed. When these double doors were shut and all other entrances were closed, Babylon was impregnable. Ancient Babylon was "most proud," "a golden cup ... that made all the earth drunken ... of her wine." Jeremiah 50:32; 51:7. Yet she was to fall suddenly and be destroyed (Jeremiah 51:8). Then God would call Israel, saying, "My people, go ye out of the midst of her." Jeremiah 51:45. As we shall soon see, these exact words are repeated in the book of Revelation to spiritual Israel about the importance of coming out of modern Babylon (Revelation 17:4,5; 18:2-8).

In 538 B.C., on the night of ancient Babylon's fall, her king and subjects were drunk with wine (Daniel chapter 5). So were the guards, and they forgot to fully close the double doors. Over 100 years earlier, God had predicted concerning Babylon and the Euphrates, "I will dry up thy rivers." Isaiah 44:27. The Lord also spoke about "Cyrus," who conquered Babylon, saying, "I will

... open before him the two leaved gates; and the gates shall not be shut." Isaiah 45:1. Moreover God called Cyrus "my shepherd" and "his anointed" (Isaiah 44:28; 45:1). Thus Cyrus was a type of Jesus Christ. And he came "from the east" Isaiah 46:11!

Inside the British Museum in London lies the famous Cyrus Cylinder. It describes how Cyrus, a general of Darius, conquered Babylon. Cyrus and his army dug trenches upstream alongside of the river Euphrates. By diverting the water, the river gradually went down as it ran through the city of Babylon. No one noticed. At night, at the height of Belshazzar's drunken feast, the water became low enough for Cyrus and his men to quietly slip under the double doors, which had been left open. Quickly they overran the doomed city, killed the king (Daniel 5:30), and conquered Babylon. Then Cyrus issued a decree to let Israel go (Ezra chapter 1).

The book of Revelation uses the events, geography, and terminology of the Old Testament, and then applies them universally to Jesus Christ, the Israel of God, and modern Babylon at the end of time. A failure to discern this principle has resulted in a massive misunderstanding of Revelation, a false Middle-East focus, *and deception!*

In Revelation chapter 17, a holy angel said to the apostle John: "Come hither; I will shew unto thee the judgment of the great whore that sitteth upon many waters." "So he carried me away in the spirit into the wilderness: and I saw a woman sit upon a scarlet coloured beast, full of names of blasphemy, ... having a golden cup in her hand." "And upon her forehead was a name written, MYSTERY, BABYLON THE GREAT, THE MOTHER OF HARLOTS AND ABOMI-NATIONS OF THE EARTH." Revelation 17:1, 3, 4, 5. John saw this woman when he was "in the spirit." Even so must we be "in the Spirit" in order to understand this prophecy!

Notice carefully. John saw a Mystery Babylon who "sitteth upon many waters." She also has "a golden cup," just like we read in Jeremiah! Yet this "Mystery Babylon" is not the same as the ancient city of Babylon in the Middle East. And the "many waters" that she sits upon certainly do not refer to the literal river Euphrates that today trickles through modern Iraq. No! Revelation's angel interpreter said, "The waters which thou sawest, where the whore sitteth, *are peoples, and multitudes, and nations, and tongues*." Revelation 17:15, emphasis added.

The genius of Revelation is that it uses the history of the Old Testament and then applies it spiritually to a Mystery Babylon, which now sits upon the "many waters" of a spiritual river Euphrates! According to the angel interpreter, this river of "many waters" actually represents "peoples, and multitudes, and nations" around the world that support Mystery Babylon and her global deceptions (Revelation 17:15; 18:23). Echoing the ancient words of the prophet Jeremiah, yet applying them spiritually and globally, Revelation says, "Babylon is fallen, is fallen, that great city, because she made all nations drink of the wine of the wrath of her fornication." Revelation 14:8.

The error of those who adopt the "literal Middle East" method of interpreting Revelation's prophecies stems from: (1) the belief that those prophecies must apply to the Israel of the flesh, (2) a failure to study the Old Testament's "root history" behind Revelation's prophecies, and (3) a failure to apply that history spiritually and universally to the Israel in the Spirit and to the Lord's global enemies. Modern interpreters usually apply the words "Babylon," "Euphrates," and "kings of the east" to a literal city, a literal river, and literal armies in the Middle East. Yet Revelation speaks of that "which spiritually is called Sodom and Egypt," about a "Mystery, Babylon," and about "waters" that *represent* "peoples, and multitudes, and nations, and tongues." Revelation 11:8; 17:1, 5, 15.

This issue can be compared to the wearing of two different pairs of glasses. If we put on the "literal Middle East glasses" and then read Revelation, we will "see" these prophecies as applying to the Israel in the flesh. But if we put on the "Middle East *symbolism* glasses" and then read Revelation, we will "see" these prophecies as applying to the Israel in the Spirit. Paul wrote to Christians, "But ye are not in the flesh, but in the Spirit." Romans 8:9. If we put on the wrong glasses and interpret prophecy according to the flesh, we will end up more blind than a bat. But if we put on the right glasses and interpret prophecy according to the Spirit, then we will say, "I was blind, now I see." John 9:25.

A woman in prophecy represents a church. The Church of Jesus Christ is called "his wife" who makes "herself ready" for the marriage supper of the Lamb (Revelation 19:7, 8). That woman called "MYSTERY, BABYLON" represents a false form of Christianity which has fallen away from God and is now leading "peoples, and multitudes, and nations, and tongues" away from the truth of Jesus Christ! Just like ancient Israel during her darkest days, this modern Babylon is now "playing the harlot." Ezekiel 16:1, 2, 15, 35. She is even now making "all nations" drunk with "her wine," which represents her false doctrines. This Mystery Babylon is now denying "the mystery of Christ" that we studied about in Chapter 7. She has rebuilt a wall between Jews and Gentiles—a wall that Jesus Christ abolished at the cross (Ephesians 2:14-17).

In the Old Testament, when Cyrus dried up the *literal* river Euphrates, God told *literal* Jews to come out of *literal* Babylon. "My people," the Lord pleaded, "go ye out of the midst of her, and deliver ye every man his soul from the fierce anger of the Lord." Jeremiah 51:45. This very same call is now being given in

Revelation to those in the midst of *spiritual* Babylon. God says, "Come out of her, my people, that ye be not partakers of her sins, and that ye receive not of her plagues." Revelation 18:4.

Inside spiritual Babylon today are large numbers of true Christians who are serving the Lord to the best of their ability. This applies to many who are even now teaching false prophecy. Yet God still calls them "my people." The Lord mercifully sees them as part of His spiritual Israel. But they are confused! The word "Babylon" means "confusion." Because of today's global religious confusion, especially about Bible prophecy, millions of the Lord's people now believe false theories about the end of time! Yet according to Revelation 18:4, Jesus Christ is now calling us all to "come out" of spiritual confusion and *into the truth of His Word.* We must all leave Babylon before it is too late! Soon the river will run dry!

"The sixth angel poured out his vial upon the great river Euphrates; and the water thereof was *dried up."* Revelation 16:12, emphasis added. "Babylon the Great" now sits on "the great river Euphrates." This river represents "peoples, and multitudes" around the world who, refusing to come out, continue to support the false doctrines of Mystery Babylon. Soon "the sixth angel" will pour out "his vial upon the great river Euphrates." This vial is one of the seven "vials of the wrath of God." Revelation 16:1. Thus, it is the wrath of God, not modern Turkey, that will dry up the Euphrates! What does it mean? Brace yourself. It means that God's wrath will be soon poured out upon *people* who continue to support the deceptions of Babylon!

When the "peoples, and multitudes, and nations" that have supported modern Babylon up to the end finally experience God's wrath, then they will realize that they have been deceived. Then they will "hate the whore, and shall make her desolate and naked, and shall eat her flesh, and burn her with fire." Revelation 17:16. Their support for Babylon will vanish. *This is how Babylon's water will dry up,* preparing the way for the "kings of the east." Revelation 16:12.

Cyrus came from "the east" to conquer ancient Babylon (Isaiah 44:26-28; 46:11). The word "east" means "sun rising." The name "Cyrus" means "sun." Cyrus was a type of Jesus Christ, "the Sun of righteousness." Malachi 4:2. In Revelation, God's angels come from the east (Revelation 7:2). Jesus said, "As the lightening cometh out of *the east,* and shineth even unto the west; so shall also the coming of the Son of man be." Matthew 24:27, emphasis added. Jesus is coming from the east with the armies of heaven as "KING OF KINGS, AND LORD OF LORDS." Revelation 19:14, 16. Thus, the "kings of the east" are not the Chinese, but King Jesus and His armies, which will soon descend from the eastern skies to conquer modern Babylon and to deliver Israel at Armageddon!

Which Israel will Jesus deliver? It will surely be an Israel in the Spirit, which, having chosen to walk in the Spirit and to interpret prophecy according to the Spirit, has also chosen to "come out" of Mystery Babylon and to forsake its fleshy ideas (Galatians 5:16, 25; Revelation 18:4). Let's be part of that Israel!

---

[1]*Endtime* Magazine, January/February 1998, p. 2.

CHAPTER 11

$\mathcal{F}$ROGS, FABLES, AND ARMAGEDDON

Most people don't like frogs, but I used to catch a lot of them when I was a boy. Did you know that the book of Revelation talks about frogs? Amazingly, it connects them with the battle of Armageddon.

John wrote, "I saw three unclean spirits like frogs come out of the mouth of the dragon, and out of the mouth of the beast, and out of the mouth of the false prophet. For they are the spirits of devils, working miracles, which go forth unto the kings of the earth and of the whole world, to gather them to the battle of that great day of God Almighty." "And he gathered them together into a place called in the Hebrew tongue Armageddon." Revelation 16:13, 14, 16. The dragon, the beast, and the false prophet represent the three parts of Mystery Babylon (verse 19). A careful reading of this passage reveals that Armageddon has to do with a final global battle between these three froglike spirits, the kings of the whole world, and God Almighty!

The third of those "three unclean spirits like frogs" is described as coming "out of the mouth of the false prophet" and going to "the whole world" prior to Armageddon (verses 13, 14, 16). What could this highly symbolic language about a froglike spirit speaking globally through a false prophet represent? Could it represent a worldwide system of false prophecy that is now deceiving millions into thinking that Armageddon is only a Middle East conflict that does not involve them?

A plague of frogs was one of the 10 plagues of Egypt. The Bible says, "Aaron stretched out his hand over the waters of Egypt; and the frogs came up, and covered the land of Egypt." Exodus 8:6. This incident forms the background for Revelation 16:13. In the Old Testament, the frogs came up from "the waters of Egypt." In Revelation 16:12, 13, the three frogs come up from "the great river Euphrates," whose waters represent the "peoples, and multitudes, and nations" that support Mystery Babylon. The *third frog* speaking through the false prophet represents a gigantic system of false prophecy that even now covers the land.

The *third frog of false prophecy* is now teaching a literal Middle East Armageddon involving the literal river Euphrates, China, Russia, the Jewish nation, and a rebuilt third temple in old Jerusalem. Dear friend, this is all false prophecy. It is part of "the wine" of Babylon, which deceives all nations (Revelation 14:8; 18:23). The apostle Paul plainly predicted that the time would come when the majority would "turn away their ears from the truth, and shall be turned unto fables." 2 Timothy 4:3, 4. Yes, we are now living in a time of frogs and fables!

Have you read the fable of a handsome prince who was turned into a frog? What a disaster! Yet this frog-prince still had the power of speech. One day the unfortunate frog-prince happened to meet a beautiful princess. He opened his mouth, spoke, and convinced the maiden to give him a kiss. Then, presto! The frog became a prince again! What is the moral of this story for us today? The moral is that if we have come under the subtle influence of frogs and fables, it is high time to be turned back into a prince! We need the kiss of royalty. The Bible says, "Kiss the Son." Psalm 2:12. Through the words of truth that fall from the lips of King Jesus, we can be delivered from the third frog of false prophecy!

"And he gathered them together into a place called in the Hebrew tongue Armageddon." Revelation 16:16. This is the only time the word "Armageddon" is used in the Bible. The truth is that there is no literal place called "Armageddon" anywhere in the world. This mysterious word is a combination of two words: (1) "Ar," which means "mountain," and (2) "Mageddon," which reminds us of the ancient valley of Megiddo

(2 Chronicles 35:22). In the Old Testament, the valley of Megiddo was a place of bloody battles and great slaughters. Thus, the mysterious word "Armageddon" suggests a mountain of slaughter.

In Bible prophecy, the word "mountain" is used symbolically to refer to the global kingdom of God that will one day "fill the whole earth" (Daniel 2:35, 44, 45). In Revelation 16:14, we read about a global gathering of "the kings of the earth and of the whole world" to a final battle. These worldwide forces of Satan compose his global kingdom. They will all be gathered to "Armageddon," to the Mountain of Slaughter. Thus, we conclude that "Armageddon" refers to a worldwide battle in which Satan's global kingdom will finally be slaughtered by the approaching kingdom of God Almighty!

The actual slaughter of Satan's global kingdom is described immediately after the word "Armageddon" is used. Revelation 16:16-20 says: "And he gathered them together into a place called in the Hebrew tongue Armageddon. And the seventh angel poured out his vial into the air; and there came a great voice out of the temple of heaven, from the throne, saying, It is done. And there were voices, and thunders, and lightnings; and there was a great earthquake, such as was not since men were upon the earth, so mighty an earthquake, and so great. And the great city was divided into three parts, and the cities of the nations fell: and great Babylon came in remembrance before God, to give unto her the cup of the wine of the fierceness of his wrath. And every island fled away, and the mountains were not found." Contrary to the popular teaching of the third frog, these words clearly describe divine wrath upon Babylon and a global slaughter that reaches far beyond the geography of the Middle East!

Prior to Armageddon, the three froglike spirits "go forth unto the kings of the earth and of the whole world, to gather them to the battle of that great day of God Almighty." Revelation 16:14. This same gathering is described in Revelation chapter 19. John wrote, "I saw the beast, and the kings of the earth, and their armies, gathered together to make war against him that sat on the horse, and against his army." Revelation 19:19. Thus, the gathering for Armageddon is a gathering of the world forces of Mystery Babylon against Jesus Christ and against His army. Who will make up His army? It will be an army of angels who return with Jesus at His second coming (Matthew 16:27; 24:31).

The following passage clearly describes the actual battle of Armageddon, the victory of Jesus Christ, and the final slaughter. "And I saw heaven opened, and behold a white horse; and he that sat upon him was called Faithful and True, and in righteousness he doth judge and make war. His eyes were as a flame of fire, and on his head were many crowns. ... And he was clothed with a vesture dipped in blood: and his name

name is called The Word of God. And the armies which were in heaven followed him upon white horses. ... And out of his mouth goeth a sharp sword, that with it he should smite the nations: and he shall rule them with a rod of iron: and he treadeth the winepress of the fierceness and wrath of Almighty God. And he hath on his vesture and on his thigh a name written, KING OF KINGS, AND LORD OF LORDS." Revelation 19:11-16.

This is the truth of the Word of God. The world forces of Satan's global kingdom will soon come crashing down at Armageddon, the Mountain of Slaughter. In the midst of the ruins will lie the third frog of false prophecy. That frog will never become a prince. But you and I can! So let's turn away from all frogs and fables in order to follow the King!

CHAPTER 12

THUNDER FROM HEAVEN'S TEMPLE

He gathered them together into a place called in the Hebrew tongue Armageddon.

And the seventh angel poured out his vial into the air; and there came a great voice out of the temple of heaven, from the throne, saying, It is done. And there were voices, and thunders, and lightnings; and there was a great earthquake." Revelation 16:16-18. Immediately after the word "Armageddon" is used, the next verse focuses on "the temple of heaven." Then there are voices, thunders, lightnings, and a great earthquake. God is definitely trying to get our attention! From the context, the voice of the Almighty is now saying to us, "Look up" toward the temple in heaven!

The *third* frog is now telling us to look down toward a *third* temple on earth. This is a strategy called diversion. In 1991, during Operation Desert Storm, the allies built up their forces to the east of Iraq in the

Persian Gulf. Thus, Sadaam Hussein thought an attack was coming from the east. However, the allies attacked from the west! This attack was successful because Sadaam was not looking in that direction. Today, the third frog is doing the same thing! He wants us to look in the wrong direction toward a rebuilt third temple on earth. If we follow his croaking counsel, then we will fail to learn life-saving truth that comes from another direction!

Again John wrote, "The temple of God was opened in heaven, and there was seen in his temple the ark of his testament: and there were lightnings, and voices, and thunderings, and an earthquake." Revelation 11:19. Here are the same manifestations of God's power that we just read about in Revelation chapter 16. Yet now these fireworks are connected with the seeing of "the ark" in heaven's temple. Millions have seen the movie *Raiders of the Lost Ark*. In it, Indiana Jones finds the lost ark of the covenant. That movie was fantasy, yet Revelation is reality! As a result of the third frog's strategy of diversion, the knowledge of the heavenly ark has been lost. Isn't it time to regain that knowledge?

The same manifestations of God's power described twice in Revelation also occurred when the Almighty came down on Mount Sinai to give the Ten Commandments (Exodus 19:16-18; 20:1-17). The Ten Commandments were called "tables of testimony, tables of stone, written with the finger of God." Exodus 31:18.

(See also Exodus 34:28, 29.) After Moses received the tables, he then "came down from the mount, and put the tables in the ark." Deuteronomy 10:5. Because those two tables were placed in the ark, that special box was called "the ark of the testimony." Exodus 40:20, 21.

Revelation 11:19 says, "The temple of God was opened in heaven, and there was seen in his temple the ark of his testament." Inside that ark are the Ten Commandments. This is a truth that God wants us to see! Yet the devil is determined to blind us. This is the reason for his strategy of diversion. Through the *third frog of false prophecy*, the great deceiver is now trying to divert our minds toward a rebuilt *third* temple on earth. Why? Because that temple has no ark! If we follow his croaking counsel, we will look in the wrong direction, bypass heaven's temple, and thus fail to "see" the present importance of the Ten Commandments!

Mystery Babylon has not only rebuilt a wall between Jews and Gentiles, but she also teaches that the Ten Commandments were given only for Israel and not for the Church! Yet Jesus Christ, the Author of the Church, declared: "Think not that I am come to destroy the law, or the prophets: I am not come to destroy, but to fulfill. For verily I say unto you, Till heaven and earth pass, one jot or one tittle shall in no wise pass from the law, till all be fulfilled. Whosoever therefore shall break one of these least commandments, and shall teach men so, he shall be called the least in the kingdom of heaven:

but whosoever shall do and teach them, the same shall be called great in the kingdom of heaven." Matthew 5:17-19. In these words, Jesus plainly said we should "do" and "teach" the "commandments." We should not even "break one" of them!

A few verses later, in Matthew 5:27, Jesus quoted the seventh commandment: "Thou shalt not commit adultery." Christ commented, "Whosoever looketh on a woman to lust after her hath committed adultery with her already in his heart." Matthew 5:28. Here Jesus revealed the spiritual depth of the seventh commandment, and He also applied that commandment to everyone.

A few chapters later, Jesus rebuked the Pharisees for their deceptive practice of getting around the fifth commandment. He told them, "Thus have ye made the commandment of God of none effect by your tradition." Matthew 15:6. Here Jesus stood up for the Ten Commandments and condemned others for breaking them. Yet, today many professed Christians place Jesus in opposition to the law of God. Are they really referring to the Jesus of the New Testament? Well might we ask the question, "Will the real Jesus please stand up?"

James wrote to Christians, "Whosoever shall keep the whole law, and yet offend in one point, he is guilty of all. For he that said, Do not commit adultery, said also, Do not kill. Now if you commit no adultery, yet if thou kill, thou art become a transgressor of the law." James 2:10, 11. Think about it. How can a Christian "become a transgressor" of a law that does not exist? Can a speeding driver receive a speeding ticket for transgressing a speed law that does not exist? Of course not. Speed laws definitely do exist. And if we will but slow down and read carefully the words of Jesus and of James, we will discover that the Ten Commandments still exist and *apply to Christians!*

Paul is very clear in his writings that Christians are not saved by the law, but by the grace of Jesus Christ. "For by grace are ye saved through faith." Ephesians 2:8. Again, we are "justified by faith without the deeds of the law." Romans 3:28. Yet, Paul is equally clear in those very same writings that the Ten Commandments continue to exist and have a purpose. What is this purpose? Paul declared: "By the law is the knowledge of sin." Romans 3:20. Again he said, "I had not known sin, but by the law." Romans 7:7.

The law is like a mirror. Most of the time when people get up in the morning and look in the mirror, they don't like what they see! Yet the mirror is important. We need to look at it! It is the same with God's law. If we have the courage to look into it, we may not like what we see, but this uncomfortable revelation will help us to feel our need for Jesus Christ.

As it is written, "The law was our schoolmaster to bring us unto Christ, that we might be justified by faith." Galatians 3:24.

The Bible says, "Christ died for our sins." 1 Corinthians 15:3. Yet what exactly are "our sins"? God's answer is, "Sin is the transgression of the law." 1 John 3:4. Again, Paul wrote, "By the law is the knowledge of sin." Romans 3:20. Thus, when we look at the law, we see "our sins," and once we understand "our sins," then we can understand why Jesus died on the cross! Two thousand years ago, outside Jerusalem on the crest of a hill called Calvary, Jesus Christ experienced all of our sins of breaking the Ten Commandments! "Our sins" entered His mind and broke His heart! Through infinite love for us, Jesus paid the full price for our breaking of the Big Ten. It is the *truth.* Jesus Christ died on Mount Calvary because we have broken the Ten Commandments given on Mount Sinai!

God gave "another law" on Mount Sinai that had to do with the earthly temple and the sacrificing of animals. This law involved "sacrifice and offering and burnt offerings ... which are offered by the law." Hebrews 10:1, 8. According to Paul, it was this very "law of commandments contained in ordinances" that formed "the middle wall of partition" between Jews and Gentiles (Ephesians 2:14-16). When Jesus died, He "caused the sacrifice ... to cease." Daniel 9:27. But that law of sacrifices that ceased was not the Ten Commandments. The Big Ten are eternal, were written on stone, and are now inside the ark in heaven's temple (Revelation 11:19). Modern Babylon, which means "confusion," has not only rebuilt a wall between Jews and Gentiles, but it has also mistakenly nailed the Ten Commandments to the cross!

"God is not the author of confusion." 1 Corinthians 14:33. In order to overcome the wiles of modern Babylon, we must accept the words of Jesus (Matthew 5:17-19), of Paul (Romans 3:19, 20; 7:7, 12, 13), of James (James 2:10-12) and of John (1 John 3:4) regarding the continuation of the Ten Commandments. We must look square into the Big Ten and *realize that we are sinners*. Then, losing all self-confidence, we must repent of our sins and trust fully in the blood, merits, and worthiness of Jesus Christ! Only then can we have the promise of full forgiveness for all of our sins. As it is written, "If we confess our sins, he is faithful and just to forgive us our sins, and to cleanse us from all unrighteousness." 1 John 1:9. Jesus loves us. If we trust Him fully, He will pardon us completely!

Through faith in Jesus, believers "receive the gift of the Holy Ghost." Acts 2:38. He is called "the Spirit of truth" in John 16:13. The Spirit of truth is like a miniature atomic bomb that can explode sin and deception out of our hearts! Through the Spirit's power, believers are supernaturally enabled to keep the Ten

Commandments. Paul wrote, "That the righteousness of the law might be fulfilled in us, who walk not after the flesh, but after the Spirit." Romans 8:4. The Holy Spirit also brings the tender love of Jesus Christ into our hearts (Romans 5:5). And Jesus said, "If ye *love* me, *keep* my commandments." John 14:15, emphasis added.

This brings us to the very heart of the issue that will ultimately divide God's Israel in the Spirit from Mystery Babylon. The issue is *love for Jesus Christ* that is practically demonstrated by *keeping the Ten Commandments!* In Revelation chapter 14, this very issue is symbolically represented as being shouted to the whole world by a *third angel*. "And the third angel followed them, saying with a loud voice," "Here is the patience of the saints: here are they that keep the commandments of God, and the faith of Jesus." Revelation 14:9, 12. This same issue is repeated in Revelation 12:17 and Revelation 22:13-15 (King James Version). This issue will be understood by all who overcome the third frog's strategy of diversion, who look to the right temple, and who see the heavenly ark of the covenant (Revelation 11:19).

Dear friend, the true "Israel of God" (Galatians 6: 16) will focus on the true "temple of God" (Revelation 11:19) and will keep "the commandments of God" (Revelation 14:12) through Jesus Christ. Let's not allow the *third frog* to lead us away from the *third angel's* message to a false *third temple* that has *no ark!*

CHAPTER 13

144,000
ISRAELITES INDEED

T he dragon was wroth with the woman, and went to make war with the remnant of her seed, which keep the commandments of God, and have the testimony of Jesus Christ." Revelation 12:17. "Here is the patience of the saints: here are they that keep the commandments of God, and the faith of Jesus." Revelation 14:12. Just as a "remnant" of ancient Israel came out of ancient Babylon and rebuilt a second temple (Haggai 1:12), even so will a final "remnant" of spiritual Israel come out of modern Babylon in order to keep the Ten Commandments which are in the ark in heaven's temple (Revelation 11:19).

This final remnant is referred to in prophecy as the 144,000 (Revelation 14:1-5). They are described as coming from "all the tribes of the children of Israel." Revelation 7:4. Does this mean they are all literal Jews? Millions think so. Some popular teachers liken this group to "144,000 Jewish Billy Grahams" who will evangelize the world during the tribulation. But is this right? We have previously seen that Paul wrote that Jews and Gentiles are now "one" and are part of "the same body" through Jesus Christ (Ephesians 2:14; 3:4-6). Does the last book in the Bible contradict the words of Paul? Does Revelation rebuild a wall between Jews and Gentiles that Jesus Christ abolished at the cross? Of course not.

Let's put on our "New Testament glasses" and take a closer look. The 144,000 are described as standing on "mount Sion" with Jesus Christ (Revelation 14:1). Mount Zion is where Jerusalem sits. Yet in Revelation, "mount Sion" does not refer to any mountain in the Middle East. John wrote, "And he carried me away in the Spirit to a great and high mountain, and showed me that great city, the holy Jerusalem, descending out of heaven from God." Revelation 21:10. As John was "in the Spirit," even so must we be "in the Spirit" in order to see the truth about Mount Sion and the 144,000. Paul wrote to believers, "But ye are come unto mount Sion, and unto the city of the living God, the heavenly Jerusalem ... To the general assembly and church of the firstborn, which are written in heaven." Hebrews 12:22, 23. Here mount Sion is the place where the new Jerusalem sits. It is the home of the Church. And this is where John saw the 144,000!

In the New Testament, James wrote his letter "to the twelve tribes which are scattered abroad." James 1:1. Who were these twelve tribes? In the next sentence James called them, "My brethren." Then he wrote to them about "the trying of your faith." James 1:3. Thus, these "twelve tribes," which James wrote to as a unit, were believers in Jesus Christ! In the same letter, he counseled those from among these "twelve tribes" who were sick to "call for the elders of the church" for special prayer (James 5:14). Thus, it is clear that, to James, the "twelve tribes" were part of the Church!

The 144,000 "follow the Lamb whithersoever he goeth." Revelation 14:1, 4. Thus, they are Christians who love Jesus. They are "not defiled with women; for they are virgins." Revelation 14:4. This does not mean that the 144,000 are made up of only literal, Jewish, unmarried or celibate men! No! For this would be teaching mass celibacy, which Paul called "doctrines of devils" in 1 Timothy 4:1, 3. In 2 Corinthians 11:2, Paul also used the word "virgin," and he applied it to the Church! What about the 144,000 not being "defiled with women"? This is talking about the symbolic women of Revelation chapter 17.

The atomic truth is that the 144,000 represent a final remnant *of God's Israel in the Spirit,* composed of believing Jews and Gentiles, who are not "defiled" by the deceptions and false prophecies of the mother and daughters of Mystery Babylon (Revelation 17:5). The reason Revelation refers to them as coming from "all the tribes of the children of Israel" is because, in the process of leaving modern Babylon and all deception, they have gone through a similar "wrestling experience" with the Lord as did Jacob when the Lord changed his name to Israel in Genesis chapter 32!

At the beginning of this book we noticed that the name "Jacob" literally meant "crook" or "deceiver." This name was an accurate description of his character. Jacob stole his father's final blessing from his brother Esau. He purposefully lied to Isaac three times (Genesis 27:19-24). As a result of his wicked deception, Jacob went into exile for 20 years. On his way back home, Jacob discovered that Esau was coming with 400 men to meet him (Genesis 32:6). Filled with guilt, shame, and terror, Jacob thought he was about to die for his sin.

Then came that lonely night of wrestling with the Angel of God. Finally, just before dawn, Jacob gave up on himself, repented of his sin, and clung to the heavenly messenger, saying, "I will not let thee go, except thou bless me." Genesis 32:26. Then came this response came from the Angel: "Thy name shall be called no more Jacob, but Israel: for as a prince hast thou power with God and with men, and hast prevailed." Verse 28. Through repentance, humility, and faith, Jacob overcame his naturally deceptive nature. God gave him a new heart, a new name, a new character. He had gained the victory!

That very experience that transformed Jacob into a "spiritual Israel" is a type of the transforming experience that will produce the 144,000! This is a deep thought, yet it is true. This insight is more significant than the discovery of the Titanic in 1985. And it applies to us. By nature we are all like Jacob—sinful, crooked, and deceptive. Maybe, while reading this book, you have discovered the shocking truth that you have deceived others about Bible prophecy. The thought is terrifying! The Bible says, "A false witness shall not be unpunished, and he that speaks lies shall not escape." Proverbs 19:5. Just as Esau was coming to meet Jacob, even so will God Almighty come to meet Mystery Babylon and to punish her for her lies (Revelation 18:8). Those who "love and make a lie" will be outside the new Jerusalem (Revelation 22:15). "All liars" will end up in the lake of fire (Revelation 21:8). Thus, the truth about these Israel issues is a matter of life and death!

Yet Jesus Christ loves us! On a cruel cross He agonized, suffered, bled, and died for all of our sins, including our sins of deception! Then He rose from the dead and ascended to heaven. And now, as our great High Priest in heaven's temple, Jesus Christ has given us the book of Revelation to teach us the truth! At this very moment, the Good Shepherd is pleading with us to leave the lies of Mystery Babylon before it is too late. "Come out of her, my people," is His final call from heaven (Revelation 18:4, 8). Soon modern Babylon will be "utterly burned with fire: for strong is the Lord God who judgeth her." Revelation 18:8.

This is now our night for spiritual wrestling! Yet soon the night will end. It was at the breaking of the day when the heavenly Messenger finally touched Jacob's thigh (Genesis 32:24, 25). It was then that Jacob's self-confidence was finally broken. It was then that he clung for dear life to the Angel of God. So it may be with us. According to Bible prophecy, we are even now at "the breaking of the day." Jesus Christ is coming soon! Oh, may the Master touch us now and break us! May the Holy Spirit explode all our pride! Let's cling to Jesus for our lives and say, "I will not let You go, unless You bless me!"

As with Jacob, if we humble ourselves, repent of our sins, and depend entirely upon God's mercy, the King of Israel will not forsake us. If in simple faith we cling to Jesus, He will definitely forgive us, change us, and give us a new name. By faith we can hear the Master say, "Thy name shall be called no more Jacob, but Israel: for as a prince hast thou power with God and with men, and hast prevailed." Genesis 32:28. Jesus Christ is the true Seed of Abraham. He is the Victorious One! Through faith in Him, God will cause "us to triumph in Christ." 2 Corinthians 2:14. Through Jesus, we can escape the snares of Mystery Babylon. Through God's grace, we can each become, like Jacob, a "spiritual Israel."

The Bible specifically says about the 144,000: "In their mouth was found no guile [deception]: for they are without fault before the throne of God." Revelation 14:5. Like Nathanael, they are "Israelite[s] indeed, in whom is no guile." John 1:47. They overcame Mystery Babylon, her deceptions, and her false prophecies. The 144,000 are like Jacob. They prevail over their own deceptive natures through the grace of Jesus Christ!

The above passage in Revelation 14:5 about the 144,000 finds its root in the Old Testament. "The *remnant of Israel* shall not do iniquity, nor speak lies; neither shall a deceitful tongue be found in their mouth." Zephaniah 3:13, emphasis added. Thus the final remnant of Israel will be made up of people who speak the truth. They must be one with Jesus Christ, who is "the truth." John 14:6. They must also be guided by "the Spirit of truth." John 16:13. Composed of both Jews and Gentiles who believe in the Messiah, they will be God's final Israel in the Spirit. It is my personal opinion that the number "144,000" is symbolic. Yet whether literal or symbolic, I hope we will all "be in that number, when the saints go marching in."

This book is called *Exploding the Israel Deception*. Its purpose is not to promote anti-Semitism against Jewish people, or to offend sincere Bible believing

Christians. Rather, its goal is to enlighten minds and save souls. At this very moment, the Christian church is filled with gigantic misinterpretations of prophecy which are actually out of harmony with Jesus Christ and the New Testament. For the good of all, *this explosion must succeed!*

If you have been led to believe that the prophecies in the book of Revelation apply to an Israel in the flesh, these lies must be unmasked. If you have been taught that Revelation's statements about Jerusalem, mount Sion, the temple, Gog, Magog, Babylon, and the Euphrates River apply to those literal places in the Middle East, these errors must be shattered. If you have accepted the idea that the Antichrist will one day walk into a rebuilt Jewish temple during a final seven-year period of tribulation, this false theory needs to be blown up. If sincere people have convinced you that Armageddon centers around Russia, China, and the modern State of Israel, then someone must push the button which reads, "Destroy Global Delusions." It is now time to flee from all frogs and fables!

Every one of these supposedly "unsinkable" theories will soon hit the ice at Armageddon. All such lies will go down just like the Titanic! "Abandon ship" is the cry from our Captain! "Come out of her, my people!" is the plea of our soon-coming Deliverer (Revelation 18:4). Instead of looking toward an earthly Temple Mount in the Middle East, let's focus on the